chocolate treats

Publications International, Ltd.

Favorite Brand Name Recipes at www.fbnr.com

D1401464

Copyright © 2002 Publications International, Ltd.
Recipes, text, photographs and illustrations copyright © 2002
International Masters Publishers AB.
All rights reserved. This publication may not be reproduced or quoted in
whole or in part by any means whatsoever without written permission from:

Louis Weber, CEO
Publications International, Ltd.
7373 North Cicero Avenue
Lincolnwood, IL 60712

Permission is never granted for commercial purposes.

Pictured on the front cover *(clockwise from top left):* Fudge Dream Bars *(page 66),*
Chocolate Raspberry Tartlet *(page 46),* Chocolate Chip Pie *(page 44)* and White
Chocolate Mousse Parfaits *(page 76).*

Pictured on the back cover *(clockwise from top left):* Mint Chocolate Nougats
(page 118), Cream-Filled Chocolate Cake *(page 12),* Brownie Ice Cream Sandwich
(page 58) and Chocolate-Swirled Strawberries *(page 98).*

ISBN: 0-7853-7113-3

Library of Congress Control Number: 2002105950

Manufactured in China.

8 7 6 5 4 3 2 1

Contents

Chocolate Basics

FOR THE LOVE OF CHOCOLATE

If you're a chocolate lover, you're probably looking for the richest, gooiest chocolate recipe you can find: deliciously dense layer cakes, warm chunky cookies, super-moist brownies, creamy puddings...the possibilities are endless! You'll find all the chocolate recipes you need in *Chocolate Treats,* from simple homey desserts to more elaborate goodies perfect for gift-giving or entertaining. Easy-to-follow directions and helpful how-to photos make it easy to create these beautiful chocolate desserts. To make working with chocolate even easier, read through the following information before starting.

WHAT IS CHOCOLATE?

Pure chocolate: This is a thick paste made when the seeds of the cocoa bean are heated and ground. All baking and eating chocolates start with pure chocolate.

Cocoa butter: This is the fat that is extracted from pure chocolate and then returned in varying amounts depending on the manufacturer and type of chocolate being made. Cocoa butter gives eating chocolate its characteristic smooth texture.

TYPES OF CHOCOLATE

Unsweetened chocolate: Also called bitter or baking chocolate, this is pure chocolate with no sugar or flavorings added. It is used only in baking and is commonly packaged in individually wrapped 1-ounce squares.

Bittersweet chocolate: This is pure chocolate with some sugar added. It is available in specialty food shops and some supermarkets, packaged in bars or 1-ounce squares. If unavailable, substitute half unsweetened chocolate and half semisweet chocolate.

Semisweet chocolate: This is pure chocolate combined with extra cocoa butter and sugar. It is sold in a variety of forms, including 1-ounce squares, bars, chips and chunks.

Milk chocolate: This is pure chocolate with sugar, extra cocoa butter and milk solids added. It is available in various shapes—bars, chips, stars, etc.

White chocolate: This is not considered real chocolate since most or all of the cocoa butter has been removed and replaced by another vegetable fat. It contains no pure chocolate. White chocolate is available in bars, blocks, chips and chunks.

Unsweetened cocoa powder: This is formed by extracting most of the cocoa butter from pure chocolate and grinding the remaining chocolate solids into a powder. Since most of the cocoa butter is removed, it is low in fat. It contains no additives. It is either natural (nonalkalized) or processed with an alkali to neutralize the natural acidity (also called Dutch process). Alkalized cocoa looks darker and has a milder flavor than nonalkalized cocoa.

MELTING CHOCOLATE

Make sure the container and utensils you use for melting are completely dry. Even a tiny drop of moisture can cause the chocolate to tighten or "seize" (become stiff, grainy and coarse-textured). If this happens, add $1/2$ teaspoon shortening (not butter or margarine) for each ounce of chocolate and stir until smooth. (The additional shortening will not affect your recipe.) Some recipes call for melting chocolate with liquids. It is a matter of proportions: a lot of liquid will not tighten the chocolate, but a little will. To help prevent tightening, when a recipe calls for a large amount of liquid to be added to melted chocolate, pour in all the liquid at once and then stir.

In general, be careful when melting chocolate, as chocolate scorches easily and once scorched cannot be used. Follow one of these three methods for successful melting.

Double boiler: Place the chocolate in the top of a double boiler or in a bowl over hot, not boiling, water; stir until smooth. (Boiling water  produces steam, which can turn to water and cause the chocolate to seize.)

Direct heat: Place the chocolate in a heavy saucepan over very low heat. Stir constantly and remove from the heat as soon as the chocolate melts.

Microwave oven: Place an unwrapped 1-ounce square or 1 cup of chips in a small microwavable bowl. Microwave on HIGH 1 to $1/2$ minutes,  stirring after 1 minute. Stir the chocolate at 30-second intervals until smooth. (It is important to stir microwaved chocolate since it retains its original shape even when melted.)

Water bath: If you only have a small amount of chocolate to melt (no more than 2 ounces), place the pieces in a small bowl or custard  cup and set the bowl in a shallow pan of hot water. Stir until the chocolate is melted.

STORING CHOCOLATE

Chocolate should be stored, tightly wrapped, in a cool, dry place, between 60° and 70°F. If stored at room temperature, the cocoa butter melts, rises to the surface and resolidifies. This causes the chocolate to develop a "bloom," or a pale gray film on the surface. If stored in a damp place, the chocolate can form tiny gray sugar crystals on top. These conditions only affect the appearance, not the flavor, of the chocolate. The rich brown color will return when the chocolate is melted.

CHOCOLATE EXTRAS

Make your desserts extra-special with these simple chocolate garnishes.

Grated Chocolate

Working over waxed paper, rub chocolate across the rough surface of a grater.

Chocolate Curls

Pull a vegetable peeler across a square of chocolate to create curls. Place them on a waxed paper-lined baking sheet and refrigerate about 15 minutes or until firm.

Chocolate Drizzle

Fill a small plastic food storage bag about half full with melted chocolate; seal the bag securely. Cut a very small corner off the bottom of the bag with scissors. Gently squeeze the bag and pipe chocolate directly onto desserts.

Chocolate-Dipped Fruits or Nuts

If using fresh fruit, wash and dry well. Dip fruit or nuts, one at a time, into melted chocolate until the chocolate coating comes about two-thirds up the side. Allow excess chocolate to drip off. Place on waxed paper; let stand in a cool, dry place until chocolate is firm. (Do not refrigerate.)

Chocolate Truffle Cake

What You'll Need

CAKE

1 cup plus 2 tablespoons all-purpose flour

1½ teaspoons baking powder

1 teaspoon salt

1 pound bittersweet chocolate, chopped

½ cup (1 stick) butter

7 eggs

1½ cups granulated sugar

GLAZE

8 ounces bittersweet chocolate, chopped

1 cup heavy cream

GARNISH

8 ounces bittersweet chocolate, chopped

½ pint fresh raspberries

Powdered sugar for dusting

1. For cake, preheat oven to 325°F. Grease 9-inch springform pan. Line bottom of pan with waxed paper or parchment; grease paper.

2. In small bowl, sift flour, baking powder and salt. In top of double boiler set over barely simmering water, melt 1 pound chocolate and butter; stir until smooth. Set aside to cool.

3. In large bowl, with mixer on medium speed, beat eggs 1 minute or until combined. Beat in granulated sugar until dissolved, about 1 minute. Beat in chocolate and flour mixtures. Spoon into prepared pan. Bake 50 minutes or until toothpick inserted in center comes out clean.

4. Turn off oven; let cake stand in cooling oven 30 minutes. Cool cake in pan on wire rack 45 minutes. Remove cake from pan; peel off paper. Cool.

5. For glaze, in small saucepan, melt 8 ounces chocolate with cream over medium heat, stirring until smooth. Set aside 15 minutes. Pour over cake. Transfer to serving plate.

6. For garnish, melt 8 ounces chocolate in top of double boiler. Spread thinly on baking sheet. Let stand until chocolate is nearly firm and reaches room temperature, 15 to 20 minutes. Using small metal spatula or dough scraper, scrape chocolate into loose thick curls. Let harden completely.

7. Using toothpicks to lift, arrange chocolate curls on cake. Garnish with raspberries. Place powdered sugar in strainer; tap over top of cake, dusting lightly.

Makes 16 servings

Prep Time: 45 minutes
Bake Time: 50 minutes

White Chocolate Praline Cheesecake

CRUST

- 1½ cups graham cracker crumbs
- 6 tablespoons (¾ stick) butter, melted
- ¼ cup finely chopped pecans
- 2 tablespoons light brown sugar

FILLING

- 2 cups (12 ounces) white chocolate chips
- ½ cup plus 2 tablespoons heavy cream, divided
- 3 packages (8 ounces each) cream cheese, softened
- 4 eggs, at room temperature
- 2 teaspoons vanilla extract
- 10 caramels (from a small bag), unwrapped
- ½ cup finely chopped pecans

1. For crust, grease 9-inch springform pan. In medium bowl, mix graham cracker crumbs, butter, pecans and brown sugar until blended. Press mixture evenly over bottom and 2 inches up side of pan. Preheat oven to 350°F.

2. For filling, in top of double boiler set over barely simmering water, melt chocolate chips with ½ cup cream, stirring until smooth. Remove pan from above water; cool 10 minutes, stirring occasionally.

3. In large bowl, with mixer on medium speed, beat cream cheese until smooth and fluffy, about 2 minutes. Add eggs, 1 at a time, beating well after each addition. Beat in white chocolate mixture and vanilla until blended; beat 2 minutes longer. Remove 1 cup batter to small bowl and reserve. Pour remaining batter into prepared pan.

4. In small saucepan, melt caramels with remaining 2 tablespoons cream over low heat, stirring until smooth. Remove from heat and cool slightly. Stir caramel mixture and pecans into reserved 1 cup batter until blended.

5. Drizzle caramel batter over top of plain batter in pan. Taking care not to touch side or bottom of pan, swirl blade of table knife through batter to make marbled pattern.

6. Bake about 1 hour and 10 minutes or until center of cake is barely set. Cool in pan on wire rack. Refrigerate, loosely covered with plastic wrap, about 2 hours or until firm. Remove side of pan; transfer cake to serving plate.

Makes 12 servings

Prep Time: 20 minutes
Bake Time: 1 hour and 10 minutes

Cream-Filled
Chocolate Cake

8 ounces good-quality semisweet chocolate

2 pints (4 cups) whipping cream, well chilled, divided

1 teaspoon ground cinnamon

½ teaspoon ground coriander

Large pinch ground cloves

2 tablespoons powdered sugar

2 teaspoons vanilla extract

8 ounces cranberry or red currant preserves, divided

1 envelope unflavored gelatin mixed with 2 tablespoons water

3 purchased or prepared 9-inch chocolate cake layers

Chocolate candy ornaments for garnish

1. To make ganache, heat chocolate and 1 cup cream over low heat until melted, stirring. Stir in spices; cover and chill until mixture is of spreading consistency.

4. Spread with half of cream filling. Top with second cake layer and remaining filling. Top with third layer. Cover and chill 3 hours or until cream has set.

2. Beat 1½ cups cream, sugar and vanilla until stiff. Whisk in preserves, reserving 2 tablespoons for garnish.

5. Beat ganache. Whip 1 cup cream until stiff; gently fold into ganache until blended. Remove side of pan.

3. Heat gelatin mixture until gelatin has dissolved; stir into whipped cream mixture. Place 1 cake layer into 9-inch ring form or springform pan.

6. Frost cake with ganache. Whip remaining ½ cup cream. Pipe whipped cream onto cake; garnish with reserved preserves and chocolate candies.

Makes 1 (9-inch) cake

Gran's Chocolate Pudding Cake

What You'll Need

CAKE

1⅓ cups sugar, divided

6 tablespoons unsweetened cocoa powder, divided

1 cup all-purpose flour

2 teaspoons baking powder

½ cup milk

3 tablespoons butter, melted

1½ teaspoons vanilla extract

1 cup warm water

MAPLE WHIPPED CREAM

1 cup (½ pint) heavy cream

2 tablespoons pure maple syrup

Additional unsweetened cocoa powder (optional)

1. For cake, preheat oven to 350°F. Grease 8-inch square baking pan. In small bowl, stir together ⅓ cup sugar and 2 tablespoons cocoa; set aside.

2. In prepared baking pan, stir together remaining 1 cup sugar, remaining ¼ cup cocoa, flour and baking powder. Pour in milk, melted butter and vanilla; stir until mixture is blended.

3. Spread batter evenly in pan. Sprinkle reserved sugar-cocoa mixture over batter. (This will dissolve as cake bakes, forming glaze.)

4. Pour water over batter; do not stir. (Water will sink through batter during baking, creating pudding on bottom and cake on top.)

5. Bake in center of oven 40 to 45 minutes, until top is cracked. Remove cake from oven to wire rack; cool 15 minutes.

6. For whipped cream, in medium bowl, combine cream and maple syrup. Beat on medium speed until soft peaks form. Spoon cake into dessert dishes; dollop with whipped cream. Sprinkle with cocoa, if desired.

Makes 6 to 8 servings

Prep Time: 25 minutes
Bake Time: 40 to 45 minutes

—Quick Tip—

A more flavorful glaze can be added by sprinkling ¼ cup mini semisweet chocolate chips or peanut butter chips over the batter along with the sugar-cocoa mixture.

Black Forest Cake

What You'll Need

- **1 prepared 9-inch chocolate cake**
- **3 tablespoons cherry brandy**
- **1 can (16 ounces) sweet cherries, drained and juice reserved, divided**
- **2 teaspoons cream of tartar**
- **1 pint whipping cream**
- **2 tablespoons powdered sugar**
- **4 tablespoons chocolate sprinkles**

— Variation —

Cut a 9-inch white cake as directed. Sprinkle layers with 1 tablespoon raspberry brandy; spread 2 layers with 1½ tablespoons seedless raspberry jam. Wash 2 pints raspberries, pat dry and reserve several for garnish. Beat 1 pint heavy cream, 3 tablespoons powdered sugar, 2 teaspoons cream of tartar and 1 teaspoon vanilla until stiff. Assemble cake as directed, covering the first jam-covered layer with ¼ of the whipped cream and ½ of the berries; repeat with second jam-covered layer. Top with the third cake layer; cover the cake with whipped cream. Pipe whipped cream stars around the edge and garnish with reserved raspberries.

1. Cutut cake horizontally into 3 layers. Sprinkle each layer with 1 tablespoon brandy.

2. Bring 1 cup reserved cherry juice to a boil. Blend cream of tartar with 2 tablespoons reserved cherry juice; stir mixture into boiling cherry juice.

3. Cook until thickened, whisking constantly. Reserve 16 cherries for garnish; stir remaining cherries into hot cherry juice mixture. Remove from heat. Whip cream and sugar.

4. Place 1 cake layer in 9-inch springform pan. Spread with ½ of cherry filling and ¼ of whipped cream.

5. Top with second cake layer. Repeat cherry filling and whipped cream layers. Top with third cake layer.

6. Cover cake with whipped cream and sprinkles. Pipe whipped cream stars around edge of cake; top each star with reserved cherry.

Makes 1 (9-inch) cake

Mocha Ribbon Cake

What You'll Need

CAKE

- 1 square (1 ounce) unsweetened chocolate
- 3 cups all-purpose flour
- 1½ teaspoons baking powder
- 1½ teaspoons baking soda
- 1 cup (2 sticks) butter or margarine, softened
- 2 cups granulated sugar
- 3 eggs
- 2 teaspoons instant espresso powder
- 1¼ cups buttermilk

GLAZE

- 2 tablespoons butter
- 2 tablespoons unsweetened cocoa powder
- 4 teaspoons milk
- 1 cup powdered sugar
- Strawberries for garnish

1. For cake, preheat oven to 350°F. Grease and flour 10-inch fluted tube pan. Melt chocolate in top of double boiler set over barely simmering water; stir until smooth. Set aside.

2. In small bowl, combine flour, baking powder and baking soda. In large bowl, with mixer on medium speed, beat butter, sugar, eggs and espresso powder 1 minute. On low speed, alternately beat in flour mixture and buttermilk until just combined.

3. In small bowl, combine melted chocolate and 2 cups batter with spatula; mix just until combined.

4. Pour half of remaining plain batter into prepared pan. Spoon chocolate batter on top.

(It is not necessary to smooth out chocolate batter in pan; it will spread during baking and form ribbon.) Pour remaining plain batter on top of chocolate ribbon.

5. Bake 50 minutes or until toothpick inserted in center comes out clean. Cool cake in pan on wire rack 10 minutes. Turn out cake onto rack; cool completely.

6. For glaze, in small saucepan, melt butter over medium heat. Whisk in cocoa until smooth. Stir in milk, then stir in powdered sugar. Spoon glaze over cake. Garnish with strawberries.

Makes 8 servings

Prep Time: 30 minutes

Bake Time: 50 minutes

Ladyfinger Chocolate Cake

1½ cups whole milk, divided

3 egg yolks

10 tablespoons unsalted butter, softened

8 ounces semisweet chocolate, cut into pieces

10 ounces purchased ladyfingers

½ teaspoon vanilla extract

1¼ cups whipped cream

Powdered chocolate or unsweetened cocoa powder for garnish

1. Heat 1 cup milk in saucepan over low heat until warm. Whisk in egg yolks; heat until bubbles appear.

2. Beat butter until fluffy. Melt chocolate in heatproof bowl set over boiling water, stirring occasionally.

3. Mix butter and melted chocolate until blended. Add egg yolk mixture; stir until blended.

4. Place ladyfingers in shallow dish. Mix remaining milk and vanilla; pour over ladyfingers. Let soak until liquid is absorbed.

5. Arrange half of ladyfingers in 8-inch round springform pan lined with freezer paper. Cover with half of chocolate cream mixture. Repeat layers.

6. Cover and chill 45 minutes or until firm enough to cut. Place platter over cake and invert. Peel off paper; garnish with whipped cream and cocoa.
Makes 1 (8-inch) cake

Chocolate-Rum
Soufflé Cakes

What You'll Need

- 2½ ounces bittersweet chocolate
- 5 tablespoons unsalted butter, at room temperature, plus extra for ramekins
- 5 tablespoons sugar plus extra for ramekins, divided
- 6 eggs, separated
- 3 tablespoons dark rum
- Pinch of salt
- ⅓ cup finely chopped toasted almonds
- 1 cup softly whipped heavy cream

1. Melt chocolate in top of double boiler or in bowl over simmering water. Stir until smooth; let cool.

2. In medium bowl, beat butter and 3 tablespoons sugar until fluffy. Continue beating and add egg yolks, 1 at a time. Stir in rum and melted chocolate.

3. Preheat oven to 400°F. Combine egg whites, salt and remaining 2 tablespoons sugar; beat until stiff.

4. Gently fold egg whites and almonds into chocolate mixture. Butter 6 (3½-ounce) ramekins or custard cups and dust with sugar.

5. Fill ramekins ¾ full. Place in roasting pan; pour boiling water into pan to come halfway up sides of ramekins.

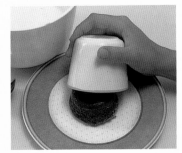

6. Bake 20 to 25 minutes or until set; cool slightly. Run knife around side of each cake; unmold onto serving plate. Garnish with whipped cream; serve warm.   *Makes 6 cakes*

Chocolate Cake Roll

What You'll Need

1/3 cup cake flour

1/3 cup unsweetened cocoa powder

2 tablespoons cornstarch

1/2 teaspoon baking soda

1/2 teaspoon baking powder

1/4 teaspoon salt

4 eggs, separated

1 cup granulated sugar, divided

1 container (8 ounces) frozen whipped topping, thawed, or 1/2 pint heavy cream, whipped, for filling

GARNISH

Powdered sugar for dusting

Fresh orange sections

Fresh mint sprigs (optional)

1. Preheat oven to 350°F. Line 15×10-inch jelly-roll pan with waxed paper. Grease and flour pan; tap out excess flour.

2. In medium bowl, mix flour, cocoa, cornstarch, baking soda, baking powder and salt. In separate bowl, with mixer on medium speed, beat egg yolks and 1/4 cup granulated sugar until fluffy, about 3 minutes.

3. In small bowl, using mixer with clean beaters on high speed, beat egg whites until foamy. Gradually add 1/2 cup granulated sugar, beating until stiff, but not dry, peaks form.

4. Fold 1/3 of beaten egg whites into egg yolk mixture. Alternately fold in remaining egg whites and flour mixture. Pour batter into prepared pan, smoothing top. Bake about 15 minutes or until toothpick inserted in center comes out clean.

5. Dust clean cloth with remaining 1/4 cup granulated sugar. Turn out cake onto cloth; remove waxed paper. Trim edges of cake. Starting with long side, tightly roll up cake with cloth. Transfer roll, seam-side down, to wire rack to cool.

6. Unroll cake; remove cloth. Spread whipped topping over cake to within 1/2 inch of edges. Re-roll cake from long side; place seam-side down on serving platter.

7. For garnish, dust cake with powdered sugar. Decorate platter with orange sections and mint sprigs, if desired.
Makes 10 servings

Prep Time: 30 minutes
Bake Time: 15 minutes

—Quick Tip—

Roll the cake while it is still warm so it won't break. Use the towel as an aid.

Chocolate-Covered Leaf Cake

What You'll Need

- ²/₃ cup butter
- ¾ cup plus 1 tablespoon sugar, divided
- 4 eggs, separated, at room temperature
- 5 (1-ounce) squares semisweet chocolate, melted and cooled for 10 minutes
- 1 cup finely ground almonds
- 1 cup sifted all-purpose flour
- 6 tablespoons orange liqueur
- 2 tablespoons apricot jam, heated, strained and cooled
- 1 cup prepared chocolate icing
- 12 rose leaves, rinsed and patted dry
- 1 teaspoon unsweetened cocoa powder
- ½ cup heavy cream
- 1 teaspoon cream of tartar
- ½ teaspoon vanilla extract
- Silver dragées (optional)

1. Preheat oven to 350°F. Grease 9-inch springform pan. Beat butter and ¾ cup sugar until light and fluffy. Stir in egg yolks, chocolate and almonds until blended.

2. Beat egg whites until stiff but not dry; gently fold egg whites and flour into batter. Pour into prepared pan; bake 45 minutes.

3. Cool cake in pan 10 minutes; remove from pan to wire rack. Prick top of cake with fork, sprinkle with liqueur and spread with jam.

4. Melt icing in top of double boiler. Holding leaves by stems, dip 1 side into chocolate; let set on waxed paper for 4 hours.

5. Let remaining icing cool; reheat to spreading consistency. Spread over top and side of cake.

6. Gently peel off rose leaves from chocolate leaves. Sprinkle with cocoa; arrange over cake. Beat cream, remaining sugar, cream of tartar and vanilla until stiff. Pipe rosettes onto cake; decorate with silver dragées.

Makes 1 (9-inch) cake

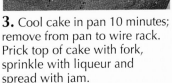

Double Chocolate Cheesecake

What You'll Need

11 squares (11 ounces) semisweet chocolate, divided

⅓ cup butter or margarine

1¼ cups chocolate wafer crumbs

2 tablespoons plus ⅔ cup sugar, divided

3 packages (8 ounces each) cream cheese, softened

½ cup heavy cream

2 teaspoons vanilla extract

3 eggs

1. Melt 8 squares chocolate in top of double boiler over barely simmering water; stir until smooth. Set aside to cool about 20 minutes.

2. Meanwhile, preheat oven to 325°F. Grease side and bottom of 9-inch springform pan. Wrap bottom and side of pan with foil to prevent leaks.

3. Melt butter in small pan over low heat. In small bowl, combine wafer crumbs and 2 tablespoons sugar; add butter. Press mixture into bottom of prepared pan to form crust.

4. In large bowl, with mixer on medium speed, beat cream cheese and remaining ⅔ cup sugar until smooth. Beat in melted chocolate, cream and vanilla. Add eggs, 1 at a time, beating well after each addition. Pour mixture into prepared pan. Bake 45 to 50 minutes or until center is almost set.

5. Turn off oven; let cheesecake stand in oven 1 hour with door slightly open. Remove wrapped pan to wire rack; cool 1 hour. Refrigerate, covered loosely with plastic wrap, at least 1 hour.

6. Remove foil and side of pan. Transfer cheesecake to serving plate. Melt remaining 3 squares chocolate in top of double boiler. Transfer to small plastic resealable food storage bag. Cut very small hole in 1 corner of bag; drizzle chocolate over cheesecake.

Makes 12 servings

Prep Time: 45 minutes
Bake Time: 45 to 50 minutes

—Quick Tip—

To form the crust of the cheesecake, use a small glass or custard cup to press the crumb mixture into the pan.

Chocolate-Cherry Layer Cake

What You'll Need

- ½ (15½-ounce) can pitted sour cherries in juice
- 2 tablespoons cornstarch mixed with 2 tablespoons water
- 4 tablespoons sugar, divided
- 6 ounces ladyfingers, crumbled, divided
- 4 tablespoons unsalted butter, at room temperature
- 1 cup plus 1 tablespoon toasted sliced almonds, divided
- ½ cup sour cream
- 2 ounces cream cheese, at room temperature
- 6 ounces semisweet coating chocolate
- 2 tablespoons cocoa powder
- Chocolate leaves (page 27)

1. In saucepan, bring cherries and juice to a boil. Add cornstarch mixture; cook and stir until thickened. Cool.

2. In small bowl, combine 2 tablespoons sugar and ⅔ of ladyfinger crumbs. Add butter; mix with hands until beads form.

3. Press crumb mixture over bottom of 7-inch springform pan; sprinkle with ½ cup toasted almonds. Top with cherries; cover and chill for 15 minutes.

4. Mix sour cream, cream cheese and remaining 2 tablespoons sugar. Spoon over cherries; spread carefully.

5. Top with remaining ladyfinger crumbs and ½ cup almonds. Melt chocolate; spread over cake, reserving some for piping. Sift cocoa over chocolate.

6. Pipe lattice pattern over cocoa with melted chocolate. Cover and chill at least 1 hour. Garnish with remaining almonds and chocolate leaves.
Makes 1 (7-inch) cake

Blue Ribbon Chocolate Cake

What You'll Need

CAKE

- 1¼ **cups boiling water**
- ¾ **cup unsweetened cocoa powder**
- 2¼ **cups all-purpose flour**
- 1 **teaspoon baking soda**
- ½ **teaspoon baking powder**
- ¼ **teaspoon salt**
- ¾ **cup (1½ sticks) butter or margarine, softened**
- 1 **cup granulated sugar**
- ¾ **cup packed light brown sugar**
- 1½ **teaspoons vanilla extract**
- 3 **eggs**

FROSTING

- 1½ **cups heavy cream**
- ¼ **cup light corn syrup**
- 2 **cups (12 ounces) semisweet chocolate chips**
- 1 **teaspoon vanilla extract**

1. For cake, preheat oven to 350°F. Grease and flour two 9-inch round cake pans. In small bowl, whisk water into cocoa until cocoa is dissolved. Let cool to room temperature, about 20 minutes.

2. In medium bowl, mix flour, baking soda, baking powder and salt. In large bowl, with mixer on medium speed, beat butter, both sugars and vanilla until light and fluffy. Beat in eggs, 1 at a time. Alternately add flour mixture and cocoa mixture in 4 additions, beating on low speed after each addition until blended.

3. Scrape batter into prepared pans. Bake 30 minutes or until toothpick inserted in centers comes out clean. Cool in pans on wire racks for 10 minutes. Turn out onto wire racks to cool.

4. For frosting, in medium saucepan, combine cream and corn syrup. Bring to simmering over medium-low heat. Remove from heat. Stir in chocolate chips and vanilla. Let stand 2 minutes or until chocolate melts, then whisk until smooth. Transfer to medium bowl; cover and refrigerate about 1½ hours or until thickened, stirring occasionally. With mixer on medium speed, beat 2 minutes until fluffy.

5. Place one cake layer on serving plate. Spread about 1 cup frosting evenly over layer. Place remaining cake layer on top. Frost top and side with remaining frosting.

Makes 10 servings

Prep Time: 25 minutes
Bake Time: 30 minutes

—Quick Tip—

To keep the serving plate clean, tuck strips of waxed paper under the cake before frosting.

Chocolate Sour Cream Pound Cake

POUND CAKE

- 3 squares (3 ounces) unsweetened chocolate, chopped
- 1 cup all-purpose flour
- ¼ teaspoon baking powder
- ¼ teaspoon baking soda
- ½ cup (1 stick) butter, softened
- 1 cup sugar
- 2 eggs
- 1 teaspoon vanilla extract
- ½ cup sour cream

GLAZE

- 2 tablespoons water
- 2 tablespoons light corn syrup
- 6 tablespoons sugar
- 4 squares (4 ounces) semisweet chocolate, finely chopped
- ¼ cup pecan halves, toasted

1. For cake, preheat oven to 325°F. Grease 8½×4½-inch loaf pan and line bottom with waxed paper. In top of double boiler set over barely simmering water, melt chocolate; stir until smooth. Remove pan from above water. Let chocolate cool at room temperature 15 to 20 minutes. (Do not chill.)

2. In medium bowl, mix flour, baking powder and baking soda. In large bowl, with mixer on medium speed, beat butter and sugar until light and fluffy, about 2 minutes. Beat in cooled chocolate until blended. Beat in eggs, 1 at a time, then beat in vanilla. With rubber spatula, stir half of flour mixture into chocolate mixture, then stir in sour cream. Stir in remaining flour mixture.

3. Scrape batter into prepared pan and smooth top with spatula.

4. Bake 45 to 50 minutes or until cake is well risen and toothpick inserted in center comes out clean. Cool cake in pan on wire rack 10 minutes, then remove from pan and cool completely on rack.

5. For glaze, in small saucepan, combine water, corn syrup and sugar. Cook over low heat, stirring occasionally, until mixture comes to full boil. Remove pan from heat, stir in chocolate. Let stand about 2 minutes or until chocolate melts, then whisk mixture until smooth. Pour glaze over cake and decorate with pecan halves while glaze is still wet.

Makes 1 loaf (16 slices)

Prep Time: 25 minutes
Bake Time: 45 to 50 minutes

—Quick Tip—

Smooth the batter in the pan so the cake rises evenly during baking and the top will be perfect for glazing.

Devil's Delight Chiffon Cake

What You'll Need

- **2 cups cake flour**
- **²/₃ cup unsweetened cocoa powder**
- **2 cups granulated sugar, divided**
- **1 tablespoon baking powder**
- **½ teaspoon baking soda**
- **½ cup vegetable oil**
- **6 egg yolks, at room temperature**
- **¾ cup strong coffee, at room temperature**
- **1 tablespoon vanilla extract**
- **8 egg whites, at room temperature**
- **1 teaspoon salt**
- **1 teaspoon cream of tartar**
- **Powdered sugar for dusting**

1. Preheat oven to 325°F. In large bowl, whisk flour, cocoa, 1⅓ cups granulated sugar, baking powder and baking soda. Make well in center of dry ingredients. Add oil, egg yolks, coffee and vanilla. Beat on medium speed until smooth.

2. In large bowl, combine egg whites, salt and cream of tartar. Beat on medium speed about 2 minutes or until soft peaks form. Beating constantly, add remaining ²/₃ cup granulated sugar, 2 tablespoons at a time; beat until egg whites form stiff peaks.

3. Stir ¼ of egg whites into cocoa mixture. Using large rubber spatula, fold in remaining egg whites in 3 additions; gently mix until no white streaks remain.

4. Gently spoon batter into 10-inch tube pan (not fluted). Bake 1 hour and 10 minutes or until surface just springs back when lightly pressed with fingertips. Immediately invert cake in pan onto wire rack or over weighted narrow-necked bottle. Let cake cool completely, about 45 minutes.

5. Gently run thin knife around pan between cake and side of pan; repeat around center tube. Turn cake out onto serving plate. Dust with powdered sugar.   *Makes 10 servings*

Prep Time: 30 minutes

Bake Time: 1 hour and 10 minutes

—Quick Tip—

Lift the beaters of the mixer to check egg white mixture for sufficient volume—the mixture should form stiff peaks.

—Quick Tip—

A bottle weighted with sand or uncooked rice makes the perfect prop for cooling the inverted cake.

Savannah Fudge Cake

What You'll Need

CAKE

- 2 cups all-purpose flour
- 1½ cups granulated sugar
- 1 cup water
- ¾ cup (1½ sticks) butter, softened
- ¾ cup unsweetened cocoa powder
- 3 eggs
- 1 teaspoon baking soda
- ½ teaspoon baking powder

FILLING

- ¼ cup caramel sauce
- 1 cup powdered sugar
- 2 teaspoons water
- 1 cup chopped pecans, toasted

FROSTING

- 1½ cups semisweet chocolate chips
- ⅔ cup heavy cream, divided
- 1 cup powdered sugar

GARNISH

- 10 pecan halves
- ¼ cup caramel sauce
- Flower petals (optional)

1. For cake, preheat oven to 350°F. Grease and flour two 9-inch round cake pans. In large bowl, combine all cake ingredients. Beat with mixer on low speed just until blended. Increase speed to high; beat 3 minutes, scraping down side of bowl with spatula.

2. Spread batter evenly in prepared pans. Bake 25 to 30 minutes or until toothpick inserted in centers comes out clean. Cool in pans on wire racks 10 minutes. Invert cakes onto racks; cool.

3. For filling, in medium bowl, mix all filling ingredients until blended. Spread filling on top of one cake layer with long, flexible spatula. Transfer to serving plate and top with second cake layer.

4. For frosting, in medium saucepan, stir chocolate chips and ⅓ cup cream over low heat until melted and smooth. Remove from heat. Stir in remaining ⅓ cup cream and powdered sugar until smooth. Cool to spreading consistency. Frost cake.

5. For garnish, dip pecans in caramel sauce; place on top of cake. Add flower petals, if desired. *Makes 12 servings*

Prep Time: 25 minutes
Bake Time: 25 to 30 minutes

Little Chocolate Cakes

What You'll Need

½ pound (2 sticks) plus
    5 tablespoons butter, at room
    temperature, plus extra for
    greasing ramekins

    Plain bread crumbs for coating
    ramekins

1 cup sugar

6 medium eggs

1 vanilla bean

2 cups all-purpose flour

2 tablespoons unsweetened
    cocoa powder

1 teaspoon baking powder

1 teaspoon ground cinnamon

¼ cup dry red wine

4 ounces miniature chocolate
    chips

6 ounces bittersweet chocolate,
    melted

1. Preheat oven to 350°F. Generously butter 10 (6-ounce) ramekins; sprinkle with bread crumbs to coat evenly. In large bowl, using hand-held mixer, beat butter and sugar until well blended and fluffy.

2. Add eggs, 1 at a time, beating well after each addition. Stir in seeds from vanilla bean.

3. Sift flour, cocoa, baking powder and cinnamon over butter mixture.

4. Whisk batter until well blended. Add wine; whisk to combine. Stir in chocolate chips.

5. Fill each ramekin ¾ full with batter. Place ramekins on baking sheet; bake 25 to 30 minutes or until toothpick inserted into center of cake comes out clean.

6. Cool 5 minutes in ramekins; turn out onto wire racks. Brush evenly with melted chocolate.
Makes 10 little cakes

Blackout Cake

What You'll Need

CAKE

- 3 cups all-purpose flour
- 2 cups granulated sugar
- ½ cup unsweetened cocoa powder
- 2 teaspoons baking soda
- 1 teaspoon salt
- ¾ cup vegetable oil
- 2 tablespoons white vinegar
- 2 cups cold water
  Powdered sugar for dusting

FROSTING

- 1½ cups granulated sugar
- 1 cup unsweetened cocoa powder
- 1 cup heavy cream
- 2 tablespoons butter
- 1 tablespoon vanilla extract

1. For cake, preheat oven to 350°F. Grease and flour two 9×2½-inch round cake pans. In large bowl, mix flour, granulated sugar, cocoa, baking soda and salt. In medium bowl, mix oil, vinegar and water. Add liquid ingredients to dry ingredients; mix until blended and smooth.

2. Pour batter into prepared pans. Bake 25 to 30 minutes or until toothpick inserted in centers comes out clean.

3. Cool cakes in pans on wire racks. Invert cakes onto racks and cool completely. Turn cakes right side up; trim each layer to stand about 1½ inches tall using long serrated knife. Cut trimmed-off cake tops into ½- to 1-inch cubes; set aside.

4. For frosting, in medium saucepan, combine all frosting ingredients. Stir over medium heat about 2 minutes until smooth and blended. Cook, stirring constantly, 5 minutes longer. Do not boil. Transfer frosting to medium bowl; cool completely. Cover with plastic wrap and refrigerate 1 hour.

5. With mixer on medium speed, beat chilled frosting until glossy, about 3 minutes. Place one cake layer on serving plate; spread ⅓ of frosting over top. Place second cake layer on top and spread remaining frosting on top and side of cake.

6. Press reserved cake cubes into frosting all over top and side of cake, distributing as evenly as possible. Dust with powdered sugar.

Makes 10 servings

Prep Time: 30 minutes
Bake Time: 30 minutes

Chocolate Chip Pie

What You'll Need

- ½ cup (1 stick) plus 1 tablespoon butter, melted, divided
- 1 cup packed light brown sugar
- 2 eggs
- ½ teaspoon vanilla extract
- 1⅓ cups all-purpose flour
- 1¼ teaspoons baking powder
- ¼ teaspoon salt
- 1 cup (6 ounces) semisweet chocolate chips
- ½ cup chopped walnuts
- Hot fudge sauce
- Vanilla ice cream

— Variation —

Triple Chipper Pie: *Omit the nuts and reduce the semisweet chocolate chips to ½ cup. Add ½ cup each milk chocolate chips and peanut butter chips. Proceed as directed.*

1. Preheat oven to 325°F. Lightly grease 9-inch pie pan. In large bowl, beat ½ cup melted butter and brown sugar on medium speed until blended.

2. Beat in eggs, 1 at a time. Beat in vanilla. Add flour, baking powder and salt; beat until mixture is blended. Stir in chocolate chips and nuts.

3. Scrape dough into prepared pan. Flatten and smooth top with wooden spoon. Bake 30 to 40 minutes or until toothpick inserted in center comes out clean. Remove pie from oven; brush remaining 1 tablespoon melted butter over top. Set pie on wire rack to cool slightly.

4. Gently heat fudge sauce in heavy saucepan over low heat. Cut warm pie into wedges. Top each serving with scoop of ice cream and warm fudge sauce.

Makes 8 servings

Prep Time: 25 minutes
Bake Time: 30 to 40 minutes

—Quick Tips—

Brushing the pie with melted butter after baking adds extra richness and softens the crust on top of the pie.

Beating eggs into a batter one at a time helps ensure maximum volume and also helps to avoid overmixing.

Chocolate Raspberry Tartlets

What You'll Need

- **1 ready-to-use refrigerated pie crust**
- **1 cup (6 ounces) semisweet chocolate chips**
- **¼ cup water**
- **2 tablespoons butter**
- **¼ cup powdered sugar, plus extra for dusting**
- **1 pint fresh raspberries**
- **1 square (1 ounce) semisweet chocolate for garnish**

1. Preheat oven to 425°F. Lightly grease four 3×1-inch tart pans with removable bottoms. Place pie crust on work surface. Using 4-inch round cookie cutter, cut out 4 pastry circles.

2. Press each circle into bottom and up side of prepared tart pan. Place pans on baking sheet; bake 10 to 13 minutes or until pastry is pale golden brown. Transfer tarts in pans to wire rack to cool completely.

3. Meanwhile, in heavy medium saucepan, heat chocolate chips, water and butter over low heat, stirring until mixture is melted and smooth. Remove pan from heat; stir in powdered sugar until blended and smooth.

4. Set chocolate mixture aside about 30 minutes, until cool but still pourable. Pour chocolate mixture into tart shells, dividing equally.

5. Gently press raspberries, stem sides down, into filling in concentric pattern. Refrigerate tarts about 1 hour or until filling is set.

6. To serve, remove sides and bottoms of tart pans; place tarts on serving plates. Let stand at room temperature 10 minutes before serving. Meanwhile, using sharp vegetable peeler, shave strips from chocolate onto sheet of waxed paper. (Chill chocolate if curls don't form.) Garnish tarts with chocolate curls. Dust with powdered sugar. *Makes 4 servings*

Prep Time: 30 minutes
Bake Time: 10 to 13 minutes

Chocolate Banana
Cream Pie

What You'll Need

- ½ cup unsweetened cocoa powder
- ¼ cup cornstarch
- 2 cups milk
- 1⅔ cups heavy cream, divided
- ⅔ cup packed light brown sugar
- 3 egg yolks
- 1 teaspoon vanilla extract
- 1 teaspoon rum extract (optional)
- 3 ripe medium bananas, divided
- 1 prepared graham cracker crust (9-inch)
- 2 tablespoons powdered sugar
- Semisweet chocolate for garnish

1. In heavy medium saucepan, blend cocoa and cornstarch. Gradually whisk in milk and ⅔ cup cream until smooth. Whisk in brown sugar. Bring to a boil over medium heat, stirring often; boil 1 minute.

2. In small bowl, beat egg yolks. Whisk 1 cup milk mixture into egg yolks, then pour egg yolks back into milk mixture in pan. Bring to a boil, whisking constantly. Boil 1 minute. Whisk in vanilla and rum extract. Remove from heat; cover surface with waxed paper. Let cool 20 minutes.

3. Thinly slice 2 bananas; place in bottom of crust. Pour custard into crust. Refrigerate at least 3 hours or overnight.

4. In medium bowl, with mixer on high speed, whip remaining 1 cup cream with powdered sugar until stiff peaks form. Place in pastry bag fitted with star tip and pipe rosettes onto pie. Slice remaining banana; arrange over whipped cream.

5. Using vegetable peeler, shave fine curls from square of semisweet chocolate. Sprinkle shavings over whipped cream.

Makes 8 servings

Prep Time: 40 minutes

Clouds-of-Chocolate Pie

What You'll Need

- 1 ready-to-use refrigerated pie crust
- 8 squares (8 ounces) semisweet chocolate, coarsely chopped
- ¼ cup water
- ¼ cup almond-flavored liqueur or water
- 4 teaspoons vanilla extract
- ½ teaspoon almond extract
- 2 cups heavy cream
- ¼ cup sugar
- Chocolate sprinkles for garnish

1. Preheat oven to 400°F. If necessary, roll out pie crust to 12-inch round. Fit into 9-inch pie plate; flute edge.

2. Line pie crust with foil or waxed paper; fill with pie weights, dried beans or rice. Bake 12 minutes. Remove foil with weights; bake crust 10 to 12 minutes longer or until lightly golden.

3. In top of double boiler set over barely simmering water, heat chocolate, water, liqueur, vanilla and almond extract, stirring constantly, until chocolate is melted and mixture is smooth. Transfer mixture to large bowl and cool on wire rack 15 minutes.

4. In medium bowl, with mixer on medium speed, beat cream until foamy. Gradually add sugar, beating until soft peaks form. Fold cream mixture very gently into cooled chocolate mixture to maintain volume.

5. Spoon chocolate cream filling into pie crust, mounding filling on top. Refrigerate until filling is set, at least 1 hour or up to 8 hours. Just before serving, garnish with sprinkles.

Makes 8 servings

Prep Time: 45 minutes
Bake Time: 22 to 24 minutes

White Chocolate Nut Tart

What You'll Need

- 1 **ready-to-use refrigerated pie crust**
- 3 **eggs**
- 1 **cup light corn syrup**
- ½ **cup packed light or dark brown sugar**
- ⅓ **cup butter, melted and cooled**
- 1 **teaspoon vanilla extract**
- 1 **cup chopped salted mixed nuts**
- 1 **cup (6 ounces) white chocolate chips, divided**
- 1 **tablespoon shortening**

— Variations —

Use just one kind of salted nut instead of mixed nuts. Substitute 1 cup semisweet or milk chocolate chips for the white chocolate chips.

1. Preheat oven to 350°F. Press pie crust into 10-inch tart pan with removable bottom. Trim pastry even with edge of pan if necessary.

2. In large bowl, beat eggs with fork until foamy. Stir in corn syrup. Add brown sugar, butter and vanilla, stirring until sugar is dissolved. Stir in nuts and ½ cup white chocolate chips.

3. Place pastry-lined tart pan on baking sheet. Carefully pour filling into pan. Bake about 40 minutes or until filling is set. Transfer pan to wire rack to cool completely, about 30 minutes.

4. Meanwhile, in top of double boiler set over barely simmering water, melt remaining ½ cup white chocolate chips with shortening; stir until smooth. Remove pan from above water. Transfer chocolate mixture to a small plastic resealable food storage bag. Cut very small hole in one corner of bag.

5. Drizzle melted chocolate in lattice pattern on top of tart. (To create lattice pattern, drizzle chocolate from side to side on top of tart. Then rotate tart 90° and repeat drizzling.)

Makes 8 servings

Prep Time: 20 minutes
Bake Time: 40 minutes

— Quick Tip —

Because the tines pull in air quickly, it is faster to beat eggs with a fork than with a whisk.

Candy Turtle
Pie

What You'll Need

½ cup chopped walnuts, toasted

1 prepared chocolate crumb crust (9-inch)

CARAMEL

1 can (14 ounces) sweetened condensed milk

6 tablespoons (¾ stick) butter

½ cup sugar

CHOCOLATE

1½ cups (9 ounces) semisweet chocolate chips

⅔ cup heavy cream

3 tablespoons butter

GARNISH

½ cup (3 ounces) semisweet or milk chocolate chips

1 cup heavy cream

1 tablespoon sugar

Walnut halves (optional)

1. Sprinkle chopped walnuts evenly over bottom of crust. Set aside.

2. For caramel layer, in medium saucepan, heat condensed milk, 6 tablespoons butter and ½ cup sugar over medium-low heat until butter melts, stirring occasionally. Increase heat and bring to a gentle boil. Boil about 6 minutes or until caramel mixture is thick as pudding, stirring constantly. Pour over walnuts. Refrigerate 1 hour or until set.

3. For chocolate layer, in medium saucepan, heat 1½ cups chocolate chips, ⅔ cup cream and 3 tablespoons butter over medium-low heat about 4 minutes, stirring until chocolate melts and mixture is smooth. Pour chocolate mixture over caramel layer; refrigerate 1 hour or until filling is set.

4. For garnish, in top of double boiler (or glass bowl) set over barely simmering water, melt ½ cup chocolate chips; stir until smooth. Remove pan from above water. Following mold directions, fill small decorative molds using spoon; freeze about 30 minutes or until chocolate is firm. Use tip of sharp knife to unmold candies.

5. Just before serving, in medium bowl, with mixer on medium-high speed, beat 1 cup cream and 1 tablespoon sugar until stiff peaks form when beaters are lifted. Decorate pie with whipped cream, molded candies and walnut halves, if desired.   *Makes 12 servings*

Prep Time: 30 minutes

Decadent Chocolate
Pecan Pie

What You'll Need

- 2 cups (12 ounces) semisweet chocolate chips
- ²/₃ cup evaporated milk
- 2 tablespoons butter
- 1 cup light corn syrup
- 2 eggs
- 2 tablespoons all-purpose flour
- ¼ teaspoon salt
- 1 teaspoon vanilla extract
- 1 cup pecan halves
- 1 prepared unbaked pie crust (9-inch)

  Vanilla ice cream (optional)

— Variation —

This Southern pie traditionally calls for pecans, but it can also be made with walnut halves instead.

1. Preheat oven to 375°F. In small heavy saucepan, combine chocolate chips, evaporated milk and butter. Stir over low heat about 5 minutes or until mixture is melted and smooth. Remove from heat and let cool slightly.

2. In large bowl, whisk corn syrup and eggs; stir in flour and salt until well blended. Stir in chocolate mixture until completely blended. Stir in vanilla.

3. Pour chocolate filling into pie crust. Arrange pecans on top of filling in concentric circles.

4. Bake about 40 minutes or until filling is almost set. Check after 30 minutes; if crust is brown, cover edge with strips of foil to prevent burning.

5. Cool pie on wire rack. Serve warm or at room temperature with ice cream, if desired.

Makes 8 servings

Prep Time: 20 minutes
Bake Time: 40 minutes

— Quick Tip —

If you don't have time to arrange the pecan halves in circles, simply place them randomly over the filling.

Brownie Ice Cream Sandwiches

What You'll Need

BROWNIES

2 cups sugar, divided

1 cup (2 sticks) butter

6 squares (6 ounces) bittersweet chocolate, coarsely chopped

1 teaspoon vanilla extract

3 eggs

1⅓ cups all-purpose flour

½ teaspoon salt

1½ pints (3 cups) vanilla or coffee ice cream, softened

GLAZE

¼ cup white chocolate chips

½ teaspoon vegetable oil

1. For brownies, preheat oven to 350°F. Grease 17×12½-inch jelly-roll pan. Line pan with parchment paper; grease paper.

2. In medium saucepan, combine 1 cup sugar, butter and chopped chocolate. Stir over medium-low heat about 7 minutes or until melted and smooth. Remove from heat. Stir in vanilla.

3. In large bowl, with mixer on medium-high speed, beat eggs and remaining 1 cup sugar 3 minutes or until double in volume. On low speed, beat in chocolate mixture just until combined. Add flour and salt; beat just until mixture is combined.

4. Pour batter into prepared pan. Bake 30 minutes or until toothpick inserted in center comes out clean. Cool brownies in pan on wire rack.

5. Loosen edges of brownies with knife and invert onto cutting board. Using serrated knife, trim edges of brownies. Cut into twelve 3×4-inch rectangles.

6. Spread about ½ cup ice cream over each of 6 brownie rectangles. Cover with remaining rectangles. Freeze until ready to glaze. (If sandwiches will not be served within several hours, wrap individually in plastic wrap and store in freezer.)

7. For glaze, in top of double boiler set over barely simmering water, melt chocolate chips with oil; stir until smooth.

8. Place brownie sandwiches on sheets of waxed paper. Using fork, drizzle glaze back and forth over tops of brownies in random pattern. Serve immediately or return to freezer.

Makes 6 sandwiches

Prep Time: 40 minutes
Bake Time: 30 minutes

Awesome Chocolate Chip Cookies

What You'll Need

- 1¼ cups all-purpose flour
- ½ teaspoon baking soda
- ¼ teaspoon salt
- ¾ cup packed light brown sugar
- ½ cup (1 stick) butter, softened
- ¼ cup granulated sugar
- 1 egg
- 1 teaspoon vanilla extract
- 1 cup (6 ounces) milk chocolate chunks (purchased or chopped)
- ¾ cup coarsely chopped walnuts (optional)

1. Preheat oven to 375°F. Lightly grease two baking sheets. In small bowl, mix flour, baking soda and salt.

2. In large bowl, with mixer on medium-high speed, beat brown sugar, butter and granulated sugar 3 minutes or until smooth and fluffy. Beat in egg and vanilla until blended.

3. Reduce mixer speed to medium; beat flour mixture into butter mixture just until blended. Stir in chocolate chunks and walnuts.

4. Using about 1½ tablespoons for each cookie, drop dough onto prepared baking sheets; space cookies about 2 inches apart. Bake 9 to 11 minutes or until cookies are browned around edges.

5. Remove baking sheets from oven; cool on wire racks 5 minutes. Transfer cookies to racks to cool completely.
Makes 1½ dozen cookies

Prep Time: 15 minutes
Bake Time: 9 to 11 minutes

— Variations —

Oatmeal-Chocolate Chip Cookies: *Add 1 cup uncooked old-fashioned rolled oats to the batter and reduce the flour to 1 cup.*

If you're a dark chocolate lover, substitute 6 ounces semisweet chocolate, coarsely chopped, for the milk chocolate. You can also substitute raisins for the nuts, or use a combination of nuts and raisins.

Fudge Almond
Brownies

What You'll Need

BROWNIES

- **6 ounces semisweet chocolate**
- **¼ cup (4 tablespoons) butter, plus extra to grease pan**
- **1 teaspoon instant espresso powder**
- **2 tablespoons whole milk**
- **¾ cup brown sugar**
- **¼ cup granulated sugar**
- **1 teaspoon vanilla extract**
- **⅔ cup all-purpose flour**
- **1 teaspoon baking powder**
- **⅛ teaspoon salt**
- **2 eggs**
- **¼ cup chopped almonds**

TOPPING

- **¾ cup prepared chocolate frosting**
- **2 tablespoons strong brewed coffee, cooled**
- **¼ cup sliced almonds**

1. For brownies, preheat oven to 350°F. Grease 9×9-inch square baking pan. In small saucepan, melt chocolate and ¼ cup butter over low heat. Stir in espresso powder, milk, sugars and vanilla.

2. Into small bowl, sift flour, baking powder and salt; whisk thoroughly to combine.

3. Transfer chocolate mixture to large bowl; stir in eggs. Add flour mixture and chopped almonds; stir until smooth.

4. Spread dough evenly in prepared pan. Bake 40 minutes. Let cool in pan.

5. For topping, transfer prepared frosting to bowl and add cooled brewed coffee. Mix until well blended.

6. Spread frosting mixture over brownies. Sprinkle sliced almonds over top while frosting is moist. Cut into squares.
Makes 16 brownies

Chocolate Peanut Butter Cookies

What You'll Need

- **2 squares (2 ounces) unsweetened chocolate**
- **6 squares (6 ounces) semisweet chocolate**
- **2 tablespoons butter**
- **½ cup all-purpose flour**
- **¼ teaspoon baking powder**
- **⅛ teaspoon salt**
- **¾ cup sugar**
- **2 eggs**
- **½ teaspoon vanilla extract**
- **1½ cups (9 ounces) peanut butter chips**
- **1½ cups (6 ounces) chopped unsalted peanuts**

1. Working with 2 squares at a time, place chocolates on cutting board. Finely chop chocolates with knife.

2. Preheat oven to 350°F. In top of double boiler, melt chopped chocolates with butter; stir until blended and smooth. Remove pan from above water and let mixture cool to room temperature, about 20 minutes.

3. In small bowl, mix flour, baking powder and salt. In large bowl, with mixer on medium-high speed, beat sugar, eggs and vanilla 1 minute to blend. On low speed, beat in cooled chocolate mixture until blended. Beat in flour mixture just until blended. Stir in peanut butter chips and peanuts with rubber spatula.

4. Drop batter by rounded tablespoonfuls onto ungreased cookie sheets. Bake 10 to 12 minutes or until cookies are just set. Transfer to wire racks to cool completely.

Makes 3 dozen cookies

Prep Time: 15 minutes plus standing

Bake Time: 10 to 12 minutes

—Quick Tip—

For an easy method of making drop cookies, scoop up 1 tablespoon dough in one spoon, then slide it onto the cookie sheet with a second spoon.

—Variation—

Mocha Walnut Cookies: *Add 3 tablespoons instant coffee powder to the egg mixture, substitute semisweet chocolate chips for the peanut butter chips and walnuts for the peanuts.*

Fudge Dream Bars

BARS

- 1 cup (2 sticks) butter or margarine
- 1/3 cup unsweetened cocoa powder
- 4 eggs
- 2 cups granulated sugar
- 2/3 cup all-purpose flour
- 1 teaspoon vanilla extract
- 1/4 teaspoon salt

FROSTING

- 1/4 cup (1/2 stick) butter or margarine
- 1/3 cup unsweetened cocoa powder
- 4 cups powdered sugar, divided
- 2 to 4 tablespoons milk

1. For bars, preheat oven to 350°F. Grease 13×9-inch baking pan. In medium saucepan, blend 1 cup butter and 1/3 cup cocoa. Cook over low heat, stirring until melted and smooth. Remove from heat and let cool slightly.

2. In large bowl, beat eggs with mixer on medium speed until blended. Add granulated sugar, flour and cocoa mixture; beat until well blended. Beat in vanilla and salt.

3. Pour batter into prepared pan. Bake 30 to 35 minutes or until toothpick inserted in center comes out clean. Transfer pan to wire rack to cool completely.

4. For frosting, in medium saucepan, combine 1/4 cup butter and 1/3 cup cocoa. Cook over low heat, stirring until melted and smooth. Transfer to medium bowl.

5. With mixer on medium-low speed, gradually beat in 2 cups powdered sugar until blended. Beat in 2 tablespoons milk. Gradually beat in remaining 2 cups powdered sugar and enough remaining milk, 1 tablespoon at a time, until frosting is smooth and spreadable.

6. Spread frosting over bars in pan. Cut into 32 bars.

Makes 32 bars

Prep Time: 20 minutes
Bake Time: 30 to 35 minutes

— *Quick Tip* —

When preparing frosting, add the milk (or other liquid) gradually to make sure the frosting does not get thin and runny.

German Chocolate
Lace Cookies

What You'll Need

- **3 ounces German sweet chocolate or milk chocolate, coarsely chopped**
- **1½ tablespoons milk**
- **½ cup packed light brown sugar**
- **6 tablespoons (¾ stick) butter, softened**
- **1 teaspoon vanilla extract**
- **¼ cup all-purpose flour**
- **¼ teaspoon baking soda**
- **1 cup quick oats**
- **½ cup finely chopped pecans, toasted**
- **Powdered sugar**

— Quick Tip —

Lace cookies spread while they bake, so it is important to space them at least 3 inches apart on the baking sheets.

1. Preheat oven to 350°F. Line several baking sheets with parchment paper or grease baking sheets. In small saucepan, melt chocolate with milk over medium-low heat, stirring until smooth. Set aside.

2. In large bowl, with mixer on high speed, beat brown sugar and butter 1 minute or until light and fluffy. On low speed, beat in chocolate mixture and vanilla until blended. Beat in flour and baking soda until blended. Stir in oats and pecans.

3. Drop batter by rounded teaspoonfuls 3 inches apart on prepared baking sheets.

4. Bake 10 minutes or until cookies spread and have lacy appearance. Lift parchment off baking sheets and transfer to wire racks. To create curved cookies, use spatula to drape warm cookies over rolling pins or bottles. Let cookies cool.

5. Carefully peel cookies from paper or rolling pins and transfer to fresh waxed or parchment paper. Place powdered sugar in strainer and tap over cookies, dusting lightly.

Makes 3½ dozen cookies

Prep Time: 20 to 30 minutes
Bake Time: 10 minutes

— Variation —

Try drizzling cookies with a white chocolate glaze instead of dusting them with powdered sugar: In the top of a double boiler set over barely simmering water, melt ¼ cup white chocolate chips with ½ teaspoon vegetable oil; stir until smooth. Set cookies on sheets of waxed paper. Using a fork, drizzle the glaze over the cookies in a random pattern. Let the cookies stand about 30 minutes until the glaze is completely set.

Marble Cheesecake Brownies

What You'll Need

- ¾ cup (1½ sticks) butter
- 4 squares (4 ounces) unsweetened chocolate
- 1 package (8 ounces) cream cheese
- 4 eggs, divided
- ¼ cup packed brown sugar
- ¾ teaspoon ground cinnamon
- ¼ teaspoon ground allspice
- 3½ teaspoons vanilla extract, divided
- 1 cup all-purpose flour
- ½ teaspoon baking powder
- ¼ teaspoon salt
- 1½ cups granulated sugar

1. In top of double boiler set over barely simmering water, melt butter and chocolate; stir until smooth. Remove pan from above water and set aside.

2. In medium bowl, with mixer on medium speed, beat cream cheese, 1 egg, brown sugar, cinnamon, allspice and 1½ teaspoons vanilla until smooth.

3. Preheat oven to 350°F. Line 13×9-inch baking pan with aluminum foil; spray foil with nonstick cooking spray.

4. In large bowl, combine flour, baking powder and salt. In another large bowl, blend chocolate mixture, granulated sugar, remaining 3 eggs and 2 teaspoons vanilla. Stir flour mixture into chocolate mixture; mix well.

5. Spread half of chocolate batter in prepared pan. Drop spoonfuls of cream cheese mixture over batter. Spoon remaining chocolate batter on top. Rap pan firmly on counter to level batters. Swirl blade of table knife through batters to create marbled pattern.

6. Bake about 40 minutes or until set. Cool in pan on wire rack. Remove foil with brownie from pan. Cut into squares. Serve or refrigerate.

Makes 2 dozen brownies

Prep Time: 25 minutes
Bake Time: 40 minutes

— *Quick Tip* —

Lining baking pans with foil makes it easy to remove brownies or bar cookies after baking. Be sure that the foil extends about 2 inches at each end.

Black & White Cookies

DOUGH

9 tablespoons unsalted butter, at room temperature

1½ cups sugar

4 eggs

3 teaspoons vanilla extract

4 cups all-purpose flour

6 teaspoons baking powder

About 6 tablespoons whole milk plus additional for brushing

CHOCOLATE ICING

3½ ounces melted semisweet chocolate

6 tablespoons heavy cream

LEMON ICING

3 cups sifted powdered sugar

4 to 5 tablespoons fresh lemon juice

1. Preheat oven to 350°F. Beat butter until creamy; gradually beat in sugar. Add eggs, one at a time, beating until each is incorporated. Add vanilla.

2. Sift flour and baking powder. Alternately stir dry ingredients and milk into butter mixture in 2 batches each, adding enough milk to form sticky dough.

3. Drop heaping teaspoonfuls of dough 1½ inches apart onto parchment-lined baking sheets and flatten into rounds. Bake 15 to 20 minutes or until golden. Brush cookies with milk after 10 minutes to brown tops. Cool.

4. Combine chocolate and cream until smooth. Combine powdered sugar and enough lemon juice to reach spreading consistency. Using pastry brush or spatula, spread half of each of 9 cookies with chocolate icing and half with lemon.

5. Using toothpick, drag chocolate icing into lemon icing to form waves; let set.

6. Spread remaining cookies with lemon icing. Pipe chocolate icing in spiral and zigzag designs over lemon icing. Place iced cookies on wire racks until set.

Makes about 27 (3-inch) cookies

Orange Brownies

What You'll Need

8 ounces semisweet chocolate, divided

½ cup (1 stick) unsalted butter

1 orange

1 cup sugar

2 eggs

1½ tablespoon orange liqueur

1 teaspoon vanilla extract

⅔ cup all-purpose flour

½ teaspoon baking powder

Pinch of salt

⅔ cup coarsely chopped roasted hazelnuts

5 slices candied orange peel, cut into pieces

— Variation —

White Chocolate Brownies: *Melt 3 ounces white chocolate and 3 tablespoons butter; cool. Beat 2 eggs, ½ cup sugar and seeds of 2 vanilla beans until creamy. Stir in 1 cup flour sifted with ½ teaspoon baking powder and pinch salt, chocolate mixture and 1 cup chopped walnuts. Pour into greased pan; bake at 300°F for 30 minutes. Spread cooled brownies with melted white chocolate and garnish with walnut halves.*

1. Preheat oven to 350°F. Grease 13×9-inch baking pan. Melt 5 ounces chocolate and butter in top of double boiler or bowl set over simmering water, stirring until smooth.

2. Let chocolate mixture cool. Wash orange and pat dry. Finely grate enough peel to measure 2 teaspoons.

3. In medium bowl, beat sugar and eggs until creamy. Stir in orange liqueur, grated orange peel and vanilla.

4. Sift flour, baking powder and salt; add to egg mixture with cooled chocolate and hazelnuts. Stir until well blended.

5. Spread batter in prepared pan. Bake 30 minutes; let cool.

6. Melt remaining 3 ounces chocolate; spread evenly over cooled brownies. Cut into pieces; garnish with candied orange peel.

Makes about 3 dozen brownies

White Chocolate Mousse Parfaits

What You'll Need

WHITE CHOCOLATE MOUSSE

6 squares (6 ounces) white chocolate, coarsely chopped

1 cup heavy cream, divided

STRAWBERRY SAUCE

1½ pints (3 cups) strawberries, divided

¼ cup sugar

1½ tablespoons cherry-flavored liqueur (optional)

1 teaspoon lemon juice

GARNISH

1 square (1 ounce) white chocolate, at room temperature

Fresh mint leaves

1. For mousse, in top of double boiler, melt 6 squares chocolate with ¼ cup cream; stir until smooth. Remove pan from above water; let stand about 30 minutes until cool and thick, stirring occasionally.

2. In small bowl, with mixer on medium-high speed, beat remaining ¾ cup cream until stiff peaks form. Fold about ¼ of whipped cream into chilled chocolate mixture. Fold in remaining whipped cream.

3. For sauce, slice about ¾ pint strawberries; set aside. In food processor, process remaining strawberries and sugar until puréed. Transfer purée to small saucepan and add sliced berries. Bring mixture to a boil over medium heat, stirring frequently; boil 2 minutes. Remove pan from heat; stir in liqueur and lemon juice. Transfer to small bowl and set aside to cool, stirring occasionally. Cover and refrigerate about 1 hour until cold.

4. To assemble parfaits, divide half of strawberry sauce among 4 parfait glasses. Spoon half of mousse on top, dividing evenly among glasses. Repeat with remaining sauce and mousse. Serve immediately or refrigerate up to 1 hour before serving.

5. For garnish, just before serving, pull sharp vegetable peeler across chocolate to form chocolate curls; transfer to baking sheet lined with waxed paper. Garnish parfaits with chocolate curls and mint leaves.

Makes 4 parfaits

Prep Time: 30 minutes
Refrigerating Time: 1 hour

⎯ Quick Tip ⎯

When making chocolate curls, use a paper towel to hold the end of the chocolate square— this provides a good grip and clean fingers.

Chocolate Chip
Cupcakes

What You'll Need

CUPCAKES

- **2 squares (2 ounces) unsweetened baking chocolate**
- **1 cup plus 1 tablespoon all-purpose flour, divided**
- **1 teaspoon baking soda**
- **¼ teaspoon salt**
- **½ cup (1 stick) butter, softened**
- **1 cup granulated sugar**
- **2 eggs**
- **⅔ cup buttermilk**
- **1 teaspoon vanilla extract**
- **1 cup (6 ounces) mini semisweet chocolate chips**

FROSTING

- **1½ cups powdered sugar**
- **2 tablespoons unsweetened cocoa powder**
- **2½ tablespoons milk**
- **2 tablespoons butter, softened**
- **¼ cup (1½ ounces) each mini semisweet and nonpareil chocolate chips**

1. For cupcakes, preheat oven to 325°F. Line 24 standard-size muffin pan cups with paper liners. In top of double boiler set over barely simmering water, melt chocolate; remove top of pan from above water and set aside.

2. In small bowl, mix 1 cup flour, baking soda and salt. In large bowl, with mixer on medium speed, beat ½ cup butter and sugar until light and fluffy. Add eggs, one at a time, beating well after each addition.

3. Alternately beat flour mixture and buttermilk into butter mixture. Stir in melted chocolate and vanilla.

4. In small bowl, toss 1 cup chocolate chips with remaining 1 tablespoon flour; stir into batter.

5. Spoon batter into prepared muffin cups, dividing equally. Bake 20 minutes or until tops are firm. Transfer pans to wire racks to cool. Remove cupcakes from pans.

6. For frosting, in small bowl, combine powdered sugar and cocoa powder. Blend in milk and 2 tablespoons butter until smooth. Spread frosting over cupcakes; sprinkle with ¼ chocolate chips and nonpareil chips.

Makes 24 cupcakes

Prep Time: 20 minutes
Bake Time: 20 minutes

―Quick Tip―

Tossing chocolate chips with flour before adding them to the batter prevents them from sinking to the bottom of cupcakes, cakes and breads.

Chocolate-Mint Ice Cream

5 ounces semisweet chocolate

1 cup whole milk

1 cup heavy cream

$\frac{1}{3}$ cup sugar, divided

1 egg

2 egg yolks

2½ tablespoons coffee-flavored liqueur or whole milk

10 drops pure peppermint oil*

10 bite-size chocolate-covered peppermint patties

Chocolate-Mint Sauce (optional, recipe follows)

*Pure peppermint oil is available in health food stores.

— Chocolate-Mint Sauce —

Heat 1 cup whole milk, 1 cup heavy cream, 5 tablespoons sugar and 4 ounces chopped semisweet chocolate in saucepan until chocolate has melted, stirring frequently. Bring to a boil; stir in 2 tablespoons cornstarch dissolved in 4 tablespoons cold milk. Cook and stir until mixture returns to a boil and thickens. Add 3 to 8 drops pure peppermint oil or to taste. Serve warm.

1. In top of double boiler set over barely simmering water, melt chocolate. In nonreactive pan, bring milk, cream and half of sugar to a boil.

2. In top of double boiler or bowl set over simmering water, beat egg, yolks and remaining sugar until frothy.

3. Whisking continuously, pour milk mixture into egg mixture; whisk until custard coats back of spoon and reaches 170°F to175°F. (Check temperature with candy thermometer.)

4. Whisking continuously, gradually add melted chocolate to custard; whisk until blended.

5. Place bowl with custard over ice cubes; chill custard, stirring occasionally. Stir in liqueur and peppermint oil. Freeze in ice cream maker according to manufacturer's directions until almost firm.

6. Coarsely chop peppermint patties; stir into almost-firm ice cream. Freeze until firm. Serve with Chocolate-Mint Sauce.

Makes 4 servings

Divine Chocolate Mousse

What You'll Need

6 squares (6 ounces) semisweet chocolate

⅓ cup water

3 egg yolks

1 cup heavy cream

3 tablespoons powdered sugar

1 teaspoon vanilla extract

Semisweet chocolate shavings for garnish

1. In heavy saucepan, melt chocolate with water, stirring until smooth.

2. In small bowl, lightly beat egg yolks. Stir 3 tablespoons chocolate mixture into egg yolks, then pour mixture back into pan with chocolate. Cook over low heat about 1 minute or until thickened, stirring constantly. Transfer mixture to large bowl; cool 15 minutes.

3. Meanwhile, in medium bowl, with mixer on high speed, beat cream, sugar and vanilla until soft peaks form. Transfer ½ cup whipped cream to small bowl; cover and refrigerate until ready to serve.

4. Fold remaining whipped cream into chocolate mixture. Spoon into 4 dessert cups, dividing equally. Cover and refrigerate at least 2 hours until firm. Just before serving, dollop with reserved whipped cream; garnish with chocolate shavings. *Makes 4 servings*

Prep Time: 30 minutes
Refrigerating Time: 2 hours

— *Quick Tip* —

To prevent chocolate from scorching, melt it in a double boiler or a pan over low heat; stir until smooth.

— *Variations* —

Enhance the flavor of this mousse by adding ¼ teaspoon almond or orange extract along with the vanilla extract. Or, for a mocha-flavored dessert, add 2 teaspoons instant espresso powder when melting chocolate in step 1.

Chocolate Bread Pudding

What You'll Need

Ingredients

4 cups milk

4 cups cubed stale or lightly toasted fresh French or Italian bread (cut into 1-inch cubes)

2 squares (2 ounces) unsweetened chocolate

2 squares (2 ounces) semisweet chocolate

4 eggs

1 cup sugar

2 teaspoons vanilla extract

½ cup raisins (optional)

½ cup chopped nuts or coconut (optional)

Vanilla ice cream (optional)

1. Preheat oven to 350°F. Lightly grease 9-inch square baking dish.

2. Pour milk into large shallow bowl. Add bread cubes; let soak about 20 minutes or until most of milk is absorbed.

3. Meanwhile, in top of double boiler set over barely simmering water, melt unsweetened and semisweet chocolates, stirring until blended and smooth. Remove pan from above water.

4. In medium bowl, beat eggs, sugar, melted chocolate and vanilla until blended. Add to bread mixture, stirring until well blended. Stir in raisins and nuts. (Recipe can be prepared ahead to this point, covered and refrigerated for several hours.)

5. Transfer mixture to prepared baking dish. Set baking dish in roasting pan. Pour hot water into roasting pan to come halfway up side of baking dish.

6. Bake 60 minutes or until knife inserted in center of pudding comes out clean. Remove dish from water to wire rack. Let cool slightly; serve warm or at room temperature. Dollop each serving with scoop of ice cream, if desired.

Makes 8 servings

Prep Time: 25 minutes
Bake Time: 60 minutes

— Quick Tip —

Oven air is very dry—baking bread pudding in a water bath helps to keep it moist.

Petits Fours Triangles

What You'll Need

- 6 eggs, separated
- 1¾ cups powdered sugar
- 1 cup (2 sticks) plus 2 tablespoons unsalted butter, melted and cooled, plus extra for greasing
- 3 tablespoons whole milk
- 2 teaspoons vanilla extract
- Pinch salt
- 1¾ cups all-purpose flour, plus extra for dusting
- 2 tablespoons unsweetened cocoa powder, preferably imported
- 1 teaspoon ground cinnamon
- 10 ounces bittersweet chocolate, preferably imported, melted
- ¼ cup unsalted pistachio nuts

1. Preheat oven to 400°F. Grease 9½-inch springform pan; dust with flour. In medium bowl, beat egg yolks and sugar until blended. Add butter, milk and vanilla; beat until well blended.

2. Beat egg whites with salt until stiff. Sift flour over batter. Add ⅓ of egg whites; fold in gently but thoroughly. Fold in remaining egg whites.

3. Divide batter in half. Stir cocoa and cinnamon into one half.

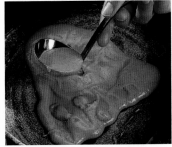

4. Spread thin layer of light batter in pan. Bake 7 minutes.

5. Increase oven temperature to 475°F. Brush thin, even layer of dark batter over light batter; bake 5 minutes. Repeat until batters are used up, alternating light and dark batters.

6. Cool cake on wire rack. Remove from pan and cut into 1-inch triangles. Glaze with melted chocolate; garnish with pistachio nuts.

Makes about 40 petits fours triangles

Festive Chocolate Fondue

- **12 squares (12 ounces) milk chocolate**
- **¾ cup heavy cream**
- **3 tablespoons any liqueur (optional)**
- **1 tablespoon vanilla extract**
- **Assorted dippers such as apple, banana or pineapple slices; citrus sections; sponge cake or pound cake cubes; biscotti or small macaroons; caramels; marshmallows; candied fruit peel; pretzels or potato chips**

— Quick Tip —

Finely chopping the chocolate (into pieces about the size of a grain of rice) ensures that it will dissolve completely.

1. Place chocolate on cutting board. Working with 2 squares at a time, finely chop chocolate.

2. In medium saucepan, warm cream over medium-high heat just until simmering. Remove pan from heat. Add chocolate; stir until melted. Stir in liqueur and vanilla.

3. Transfer chocolate mixture to heated fondue pot. Arrange desired dippers around fondue.
Makes 2 cups (8 servings)

Prep Time: 20 minutes
Cook Time: 5 minutes

— Variations —

Substitute 12 squares white chocolate for milk chocolate and reduce cream to ⅔ cup to create an especially elegant fondue—perfect for a wedding shower or New Year's Eve celebration.

For a caramel-chocolate fondue, melt 12 ounces chopped semisweet chocolate, 1 cup cream and 15 unwrapped individual caramels over low heat, stirring until melted and smooth.

Triple Chocolate Cupcakes

What You'll Need

CUPCAKES

- 1 cup packed light brown sugar
- 5 tablespoons butter
- 1 egg
- 1 cup whole milk
- 1½ teaspoons vanilla extract
- 2¼ cups all-purpose flour
- 2 teaspoons baking powder
- Pinch of salt
- 4 teaspoons unsweetened cocoa powder
- ¼ cup chocolate chips

FROSTING

- 1 cup powdered sugar
- 3 tablespoons all-purpose flour
- 2 tablespoons butter
- 2 teaspoons unsweetened cocoa powder
- 1 teaspoon vanilla extract
- About 3 tablespoons mineral water
- Sugar flowers for decoration

1. For cupcakes, preheat oven to 350°F. Place paper liners into muffin tins. With mixer, blend brown sugar, butter and egg. Add milk and vanilla; mix well.

2. Sift in flour, baking powder and salt. Add 4 teaspoons cocoa and chocolate chips; mix well.

3. Fill muffin cups ⅔ full with batter. Bake about 20 minutes or until toothpick inserted in centers comes out almost clean. Cool in pans 10 minutes; remove from pans and cool completely on wire racks.

4. For frosting, in small bowl, mix powdered sugar, flour, butter, 2 teaspoons cocoa, vanilla and mineral water until smooth and spreading consistency.

5. Spoon frosting on cooled cupcake and spread to cover tops evenly. Arrange cupcakes on doily-lined plate. Decorate tops of cupcakes with sugar flowers.

Makes 20 cupcakes

—Variation:—

Chop about 15 maraschino cherries and add to batter. Bake cupcakes and cool as directed. Decorate with whipped cream, whole maraschino cherries and fresh mint leaves.

Swiss Chocolate
Eclairs

CREAM PUFF PASTRY

- 1 **cup water**
- 4 **tablespoons unsalted butter**
  Pinch salt
- 1 **cup plus 1 tablespoon flour**
- 1 **tablespoon unsweetened cocoa powder**
- 5 **eggs**

FILLING

- 3 **egg yolks**
- ½ **cup white wine**
- ½ **cup powdered sugar**
  Juice of 2 lemons
  Grated peel of 1 lemon
- 1 **packet gelatin**
- ¼ **cup heavy cream, whipped**

—Quick Tip—

Keep the door of the oven closed while baking—opening the door will create a drop in temperature, causing the pastry to collapse.

1. Preheat oven to 425°F. In saucepan, bring water, butter and salt to a boil. Add flour; stir until mixture forms a ball.

2. Blend dough with cocoa. Add 5 eggs, one at a time, mixing well after each addition.

3. Using pastry bag with large star tip, pipe 4-inch logs of dough onto ungreased baking sheet about 2 inches apart. Bake on middle rack of oven 20 minutes. (Do not open oven door during baking.) Cut eclairs in half while warm.

4. In saucepan, combine egg yolks, wine, sugar, lemon juice and peel; stir until well blended.

5. Sprinkle gelatin over lemon mixture; let soften 5 minutes. Heat, stirring, until gelatin has dissolved; let cool.

6. Fold whipped cream into cooled lemon mixture. Let stand 15 minutes. Spoon into pastry bag fitted with large star tip. Just before serving, fill bottom half of each eclair with filling; cover with top halves.

Makes 10 eclairs

Chocolate Mousse

What You'll Need

- **7 ounces imported semisweet chocolate**
- **2 ounces imported milk chocolate**
- **1½ teaspoons unflavored gelatin**
- **1 pint plus 5 ounces whipping cream, divided**
- **1 egg plus 2 egg yolks, at room temperature**
- **1½ tablespoons Cognac or good-quality brandy**
- **Powdered sugar (optional)**
- **Fresh mint sprigs (optional)**

—— *Variation* ——

Chocolate Mousse Tartlets: *Fill 6 small purchased tartlet shells with chocolate mousse and top with fresh raspberries. Cover the tartlets and chill 2 hours until set. Garnish with a dollop of whipped cream flavored with 1 tablespoon framboise (raspberry liqueur), if desired, and fresh mint sprigs.*

1. Coarsely chop chocolates. Place in metal bowl or top of double boiler; melt over hot water. Let cool.

2. In saucepan heat gelatin and 2 tablespoons whipping cream until gelatin has dissolved; let cool. Beat egg and yolks in bowl or top of double boiler at high speed over simmering water until tripled in volume.

3. Add cooled gelatin to chocolate; stir chocolate mixture and cognac into foamed eggs until blended.

4. Set aside chocolate-egg mixture to cool. Beat remaining whipping cream until almost stiff.

5. Gently fold ⅓ of whipped cream into chocolate mixture, then fold in remaining whipped cream until no streaks remain.

6. Cover and chill 2 hours or until set. Dip spoon into cold water; scoop mousse into ovals. Place on serving plates; dust with powdered sugar and garnish with mint, if desired.

Makes 6 to 8 servings

Heavenly Chocolate Truffles

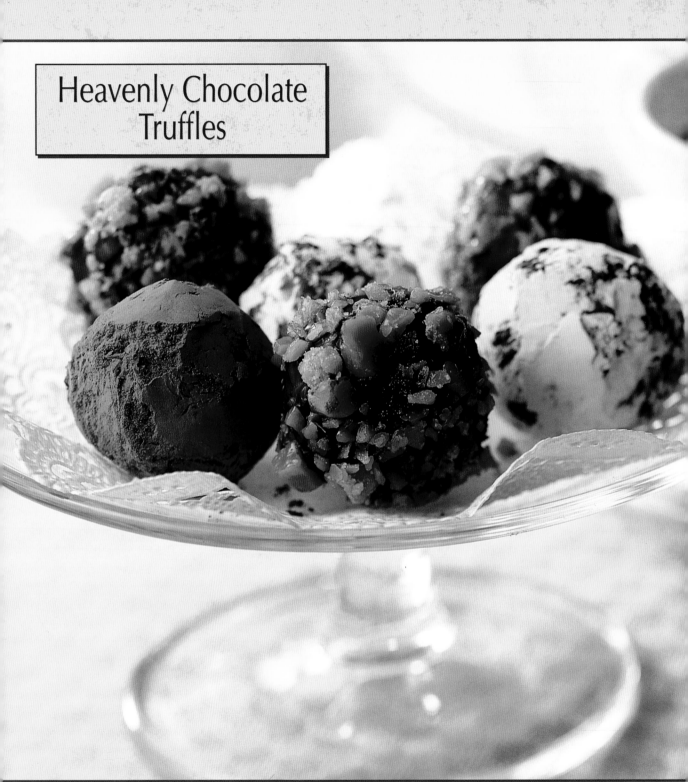

What You'll Need

TRUFFLES

¼ **cup (½ stick) butter**

¼ **cup heavy cream**

4 **squares (4 ounces) semisweet chocolate, finely chopped**

COATING

4 **squares (4 ounces) semisweet chocolate, finely chopped**

1 **tablespoon vegetable oil**

½ **cup unsweetened cocoa powder**

½ **cup powdered sugar**

½ **cup crushed toffee candies**

1. For truffles, in medium saucepan, heat butter and cream to a boil over medium-high heat. Remove pan from heat. Add 4 squares chocolate; stir until chocolate is melted and mixture is smooth.

2. Pour chocolate mixture into shallow bowl. Cover and refrigerate about 2 hours or until firm.

3. Line 2 baking sheets with waxed paper. Scoop out chilled chocolate by rounded teaspoonfuls; shape each into small ball. Place on prepared baking sheets. Refrigerate 30 minutes or until firm.

4. For coating, in top of double boiler set over barely simmering water, melt 4 squares chocolate with oil, stirring until smooth. Transfer mixture to bowl; cool slightly.

5. Place cocoa powder in small bowl. Place powdered sugar in another small bowl. Place toffee in third small bowl.

6. Using 2 forks, lower truffles, one at a time, into melted chocolate. Lift out, allowing excess coating to drip back into bowl. Immediately roll each

truffle in bowl with cocoa powder, powdered sugar or toffee. Return truffle to baking sheet. Refrigerate about 30 minutes or until coating is set.   *Makes 1 dozen truffles*

Prep Time: 30 minutes
Refrigerating Time: 3 hours

— Variations —

For orange-flavored truffles, add 2 tablespoons orange juice and 1 teaspoon grated orange peel to the butter mixture. For mocha truffles, add 2 tablespoons coffee-flavored liqueur, brewed espresso or strong brewed coffee to the butter mixture.

Chocolate-Swirled Strawberries

What You'll Need

- **4 ounces white chocolate**
- **4 ounces dark chocolate**
- **2 dozen perfect large strawberries, with hulls**

— Quick Tips —

Prepare the strawberries the day you will serve them, as strawberries are delicate and tend to lose their color and texture quickly. For an elegant gift, enclose the decorated berries in paper candy cups; pack them in a box lined with tissue paper.

To create a cone for piping chocolate, form baking parchment into a small cone shape, closing the ends of the parchment with tape. Or, cut one corner off a small resealable plastic food storage bag to make a quick tool for piping.

1. With sharp knife, finely chop chocolates for easy melting. (Keep white separated from dark.)

2. Rinse unhulled strawberries, being careful not to damage stems and leaves. Dry with paper towels.

3. Heat chocolate in top of double boiler set over simmering water, stirring occasionally, until melted and smooth. Remove from heat.

4. Holding berries at top, dip halfway into melted chocolate (white or dark). Place berries on wire rack to let chocolate set.

5. Fill piping bag or parchment cone with contrasting chocolate. Piping tip or hole must be very small.

6. When chocolate coating is hardened, hold berries upside down and decorate with contrasting swirls. Let set on wire rack.

Makes 2 dozen strawberries

Party Candy Cups

What You'll Need

CUPS

1 cup (6 ounces) semisweet chocolate chips

MILK CHOCOLATE CANDIES

½ cup (3 ounces) milk chocolate chips

¼ teaspoon almond extract

2 tablespoons finely chopped almonds

WHITE CHOCOLATE CANDIES

½ cup (3 ounces) white chocolate chips

¼ teaspoon vanilla extract

2 tablespoons finely chopped pecans

1. For cups, in top of double boiler set over barely simmering water, melt semisweet chocolate chips; stir until smooth. Remove pan from above water.

2. For each candy cup, stack 2 or 3 foil mini muffin baking cups together. Using back of spoon, spread melted chocolate inside cups, covering bottom and sides (fill all creases in foil cups). Place each foil cup in mini muffin pan cup; refrigerate about 30 minutes or until firm.

3. Meanwhile, prepare candies. In top of double boiler set over barely simmering water, melt milk chocolate chips; stir until smooth. Remove pan from above water. Stir in almond extract and almonds until well blended. Repeat process with white chocolate chips, vanilla and pecans.

4. Using small spoon, fill small candy molds just to edge with chocolate. Tap each mold gently on countertop to remove any air bubbles. Freeze about 10 minutes or until firm. Use tip of small sharp knife to release candies.

5. To assemble cups, lift foil cups from muffin pans; very gently peel foil away from chocolate, taking care not to crush chocolate. Fill chocolate cups with candies. Refrigerate until ready to use.

Makes 12 mini cups, 12 milk chocolate candies and 12 white chocolate candies

Prep Time: 1 hour 20 minutes

Rum Truffles

What You'll Need

8 ounces semisweet chocolate

4 ounces milk chocolate

½ cup heavy cream

7 tablespoons unsalted butter

2 ounces premium dark rum

8 ounces chocolate sprinkles

—Quick Tips—

To achieve the richest flavor and texture, use the finest-quality chocolates you can find, preferably imported.

When shaping the chocolate into balls, rinse your hands frequently in cold water to avoid melting.

—Variation—

Whiskey Truffles: *Prepare chocolate mixture as directed, substituting 2 ounces premium whiskey for rum. Shape into balls, dip in melted milk chocolate, roll in cocoa powder and place on waxed paper until set.*

1. Coarsely chop chocolates. Heat chopped chocolates in top of double boiler or bowl set over simmering water, stirring occasionally, until melted and smooth. Remove from heat and set aside to cool.

2. In separate pan, heat cream until hot but not boiling. Add butter; stir until melted. Let cool.

3. Whisk rum into melted chocolate. Add chocolate to cream mixture; whisk until blended.

4. Pour chocolate mixture into 13×9-inch baking pan lined with plastic wrap; spread evenly. Cover and refrigerate 24 hours.

5. Carefully remove chocolate from pan; peel off plastic. Cut chocolate into 1½-inch squares. Place sprinkles in shallow bowl.

6. Working quickly, form each square into a ball, then roll in sprinkles to coat. Place on waxed paper until set. Serve in paper candy cups or pack in decorative tin for gift-giving.
Makes 4 dozen truffles

Ultra-Rich
Hot Chocolate

What You'll Need

- 3½ ounces good-quality semisweet chocolate
- 1 quart whole milk
- 3 tablespoons sugar, or to taste
- ½ teaspoon cornstarch

— Quick Tip —

For the best flavor, use a good-quality, semisweet chocolate that contains at least 35% chocolate liquor. Check the ingredients to make sure you are buying real chocolate and not an artificially flavored product.

— Variation —

In nonreactive saucepan, whisk 1 cup whole milk, 1 heaping teaspoon unsweetened cocoa powder and 1 teaspoon sugar; mix well. Bring to a boil; remove from heat and let cool. Cover and chill. In tall glass, mix 1½ tablespoons each coffee liqueur and dark rum; add chilled chocolate milk. Sprinkle with ground chocolate. For winter, pour liqueur and rum into a mug, then fill with hot chocolate milk.

1. Coarsely chop chocolate. Heat in clean, dry bowl or top of double-boiler set over simmering, not boiling, water until melted and smooth, stirring continuously.

2. In small nonreactive saucepan, heat milk until hot; do not boil. Place pan next to melted chocolate.

3. Whisking continuously, gradually add sugar to chocolate; whisk until well blended.

4. Whisking continuously, gradually add hot milk to chocolate; whisk until well blended.

5. Bring chocolate mixture to a boil, stirring frequently. In cup, stir cornstarch into 2 to 3 tablespoons water until dissolved.

6. Whisk cornstarch mixture into hot chocolate; return to a boil. Pour into tall glasses with handles or large mugs. Serve hot. *Makes 4 cups*

Chocolate-Dipped
Fruit Balls

What You'll Need

- **6 ounces soft dried apples**
- **6 ounces soft dried pears**
- **½ (7-ounce) roll marzipan**
- **2 tablespoons Calvados mixed with 3 tablespoons apple juice or 5 tablespoons apple juice**
- **2 tablespoons pear liqueur mixed with 3 tablespoons pear nectar or 5 tablespoons pear nectar**
- **6 ounces bittersweet chocolate**
- **6 ounces white chocolate**
- **1 tablespoon vegetable oil**

— Variation —

Chocolate-Dipped Fruit: *Cut 1 pound each dried apples and pears (or other favorite dried fruit) into equal-size cubes. In alternating order, thread fruit cubes onto skewers. Separately melt 4 ounces each white, milk and bittersweet chocolate. Dip each skewer halfway into one chocolate; let set on wire rack. Then dip the uncoated half in another chocolate; let set on wire rack.*

1. Coarsely chop dried apples and pears separately. Process chopped fruit in food processor (separately) until finely ground.

2. In small bowl, combine ground apples, half of marzipan, Calvados and apple juice; blend into paste.

3. In separate bowl, combine ground pears, remaining marzipan, pear liqueur and pear nectar; blend into paste.

4. In top of double boiler or in bowl set over simmering water, melt chocolates separately.

5. With oiled hands, shape apple and pear pastes separately into balls without compressing too forcefully.

6. Using long-handled two-pronged fork, dip each ball into either chocolate; let set on wire rack.

Makes about 1¼ pounds fruit balls

Chocolate Bark
Candy

What You'll Need

2 cups (12 ounces) milk chocolate chips

½ cup (3 ounces) white chocolate chips

⅓ cup unblanched almonds, coarsely chopped (optional)

— Variations —

Press ⅓ cup sweetened flaked coconut onto the marbled chocolate before or instead of the chopped nuts. Or, press ⅓ cup candied cherries onto the marbled chocolate with or instead of the chopped nuts.

Switch the proportion of white and milk chocolate, using 2 cups white chocolate chips for the base and ½ cup milk chocolate chips for the drizzled pattern.

1. Line baking sheet with waxed paper. In top of double boiler set over barely simmering water, melt milk chocolate chips; stir until smooth. Remove pan from above water.

2. In top of second double boiler set over barely simmering water, melt white chocolate chips; stir until smooth. Remove pan from above water.

3. Pour milk chocolate onto prepared baking sheet and spread to ¼-inch thickness. Making lines parallel to one edge of pan, drizzle white chocolate over milk chocolate. Using small spatula knife, draw tip through both chocolates to create marbled effect.

4. Sprinkle almonds evenly over warm chocolate; press lightly onto surface. Refrigerate chocolate mixture on baking sheet about 1 hour or until firm.

5. Break or cut hardened chocolate bark into small- to medium-size uneven pieces. Store in airtight container in refrigerator.

Makes 1 pound

Prep Time: 15 minutes
Refrigerating Time: 1 hour

— Quick Tip —

To create a marbled effect, pull a knife through the chocolate at a 90° angle to the pattern of the white drizzle.

Miniature Caramel Chews

What You'll Need

1 tablespoon vegetable oil

6 ounces unsweetened or
  bittersweet chocolate

1 cup heavy cream

1¼ cups granulated sugar

1 cup powdered sugar

— Variation —

Rum-Raisin Caramels: *Mix 6 ounces golden raisins and 3 tablespoons dark rum; set aside. Simmer 1 cup milk and 3¾ cups granulated sugar in medium saucepan, stirring until sugar has dissolved. Stir in 6 tablespoons butter until blended; let rest 5 minutes. Add rum and raisins; stir until thickened. Proceed with chilling, cutting and wrapping as directed. For a special Valentine's Day gift, line a purchased heart-shaped box with pink tissue paper, fill with wrapped candies and tie with ribbon.*

1. Line bottom and sides of 9-inch square ceramic baking dish with parchment paper; brush paper with vegetable oil or coat with nonstick cooking spray.

2. Using handheld metal grater and working over clean, dry plate, finely grate chocolate.

3. In medium saucepan, heat cream, grated chocolate and granulated sugar, stirring until mixture becomes smooth and thick.

4. Sift powdered sugar over chocolate mixture and stir until blended. Pour into prepared pan.

5. Cover and refrigerate at least 2 hours. Using sharp knife dipped in cold water, cut caramel into 1-inch cubes.

6. Cut rectangles from clear or colored cellophane. Wrap each candy individually, twisting ends to secure. Store in refrigerator.

*Makes 81 (1-inch)
caramel candies*

Chocolate-Dipped Nut Brittle

What You'll Need

1½ cups sugar

⅓ cup honey

7 tablespoons butter, softened

½ pound slivered almonds

Vegetable oil

4 squares (4 ounces) semisweet baking chocolate

— Variations —

Peanut Lover's Brittle: *Substitute roasted peanuts for the almonds. Purchase roasted peanuts or roast peanuts yourself in a dry skillet.*

Use hazelnuts, walnuts, pistachios, cashews or a combination of nuts instead of almonds. Or, flavor the nuts with spices.

1. Line baking sheet with parchment paper; lightly oil paper. In medium saucepan, heat sugar and honey until melted and smooth, stirring occasionally to prevent sticking.

2. Stirring constantly, add butter and mix until ingredients are thoroughly combined.

3. Carefully fold almonds into sugar mixture. Cook several minutes, stirring constantly.

4. Carefully spread nut mixture evenly onto prepared baking sheet as quickly as possible.

5. Allow brittle to cool slightly. Before brittle has hardened completely, cut into pieces with sharp knife.

6. In top of double boiler set over simmering water, melt chocolate. Dip each piece of nut brittle almost halfway into chocolate; let set on wire rack.
Makes about 70 pieces

Double Chocolate Easter Bunnies

What You'll Need

Plain breadcrumbs (for pan)

½ cup (1 stick) unsalted butter

4 ounces bittersweet chocolate, preferably imported

⅓ cup sugar

3 eggs, separated

1 cup plus 1 tablespoon all-purpose flour

½ teaspoon baking powder

Pinch salt

4 ounces dark or milk chocolate, melted

4 ounces white chocolate, melted

— *Quick Tip* —

For even baking and easy handling, place the cake forms on a baking sheet before filling them with batter.

1. Preheat oven to 350°F. Grease 2 (2-cup) bunny cake forms (found in cooking or cake decorating supply stores and catalogs). Sprinkle evenly with breadcrumbs.

2. In top of double boiler set over hot water, melt butter and chocolate. Stir until smooth; let cool. Add sugar; whisk until blended. Stir in egg yolks, then stir in dry ingredients.

3. Beat egg whites with salt until stiff; gently fold into batter.

4. Place prepared cake forms on baking sheet; divide batter equally between forms. Place on lowest oven rack.

5. Bake 30 to 40 minutes or until toothpick inserted into centers comes out clean. Cool completely on wire racks; remove from cake forms. Frost with melted dark chocolate.

6. Using fine paintbrush, paint details with white chocolate; let frosting set. Wrap in cellophane and tie with ribbon, if desired.
Makes 2 cake bunnies

Miniature Chocolate Cupcakes

What You'll Need

- ½ **cup heavy cream**
- 3 **to 4 cardamom pods**
- 1 **strip orange peel**
- 1 **cinnamon stick**
- 8 **ounces fine-quality bittersweet chocolate**
- 4 **tablespoons (½ stick) unsalted butter**
- 2 **to 3 tablespoons cream liqueur**
- 3 **slices candied orange peel**
- 1 **to 2 tablespoons raw sugar**

— Variation —

Cinnamon Balls: *Prepare the chocolate-cream mixture as directed, substituting white chocolate for bittersweet. Let the mixture cool, then cover and chill until firm. Using a teaspoon, scoop out cherry-size pieces and roll into balls between your palms, dipping your hands into ice water to keep the chocolate from melting. Roll the balls in a mixture of ¼ cup powdered sugar and 2 teaspoons ground cinnamon to coat.*

1. Bring cream, cardamom, orange peel and cinnamon stick to a boil. Remove from heat and let stand to infuse cream with flavor. Remove spices.

2. With clean, dry, sharp knife, chop chocolate into small pieces. Add to warm cream; whisk until blended.

3. Set aside chocolate mixture to cool to room temperature (about 2 hours), stirring occasionally.

4. Add butter and liqueur to cooled chocolate; beat with hand-held mixer until blended and smooth.

5. Spoon chocolate mixture into pastry bag fitted with small star tip; pipe into 3 dozen foil candy cups.

6. Finely chop candied orange peel. Garnish each confection with bits of peel, then sprinkle with raw sugar. Refrigerate until ready to serve.

Makes about 36 chocolate confections

Mint Chocolate Nougats

What You'll Need

1 **egg white**

4 **to 5 drops mint extract**

2 **cups sifted powdered sugar,**
  plus additional for dusting

2 **ounces semisweet chocolate**

— Variation —

Citrus Nougat Bars: *Flavor the egg white with lemon, orange or lime extract instead of mint; prepare nougat as directed. Roll into ¹/₂-inch-thick square and cut into 2¹/₂-inch-wide bars. Place the bars on a parchment-lined baking sheet and let dry 3 to 4 hours. Omit the chocolate dip. Wrap each bar in cellophane, twist the ends and tie with ribbon.*

1. In clean, dry bowl, beat egg white and mint extract with hand-held mixer until frothy, not stiff.

2. Gradually add sifted powdered sugar, beating until mixture is firm enough to shape.

3. Dust work surface and rolling pin with additional powdered sugar. Roll nougat into ³/₄-inch-thick square.

4. Working quickly, cut nougat into cubes. Place on parchment-lined baking sheet in cool place; let dry 3 to 4 hours.

5. Coarsely chop chocolate. Melt in bowl set over simmering water, stirring occasionally.

6. Using fork, dip 1 end of nougat cubes in melted chocolate. Let set on wire rack. For special presentation, scoop nougats into paper cone made from gift wrap and lined with waxed paper; tie with ribbon.
  Makes about 36 nougats

Chocolate-Covered Coconut Candies

What You'll Need

3½ to 4 ounces (about 1⅓ cups) sweetened flaked coconut

2 tablespoons white rum

2 tablespoons powdered sugar plus extra for dusting, divided

2 ounces white chocolate

2 tablespoons heavy whipping cream

5 to 6 ounces semisweet chocolate

Candied orange peel for garnish

— Variation —

Chocolate-Coated Macaroons: *Beat 2 egg whites with 1 cup sifted powdered sugar; fold in 1⅓ cups sweetened flaked coconut. Line a baking sheet with parchment paper, then drop small mounds of the coconut mixture onto the baking sheet using a wet teaspoon. Let the macaroons dry for 2 to 3 hours, then bake on the middle rack of preheated 325°F oven 15 to 20 minutes. Let cool, then dip into melted chocolate and let set on wire rack.*

1. Process coconut in food processor or blender until very finely chopped. Place coconut in bowl.

2. Stir in rum and 1 tablespoon powdered sugar. In double boiler set over simmering water, melt white chocolate.

3. Stir melted chocolate and cream into coconut mixture until blended. Divide into 3 equal portions.

4. On work surface dusted with powdered sugar, form each third into roll about ½ inch thick; chill rolls.

5. In double boiler set over simmering water, melt semisweet chocolate. Cut chilled rolls into 1-inch pieces; shape into ovals.

6. With long-tined fork, dip ovals into melted semisweet chocolate; let set on wire rack. Garnish with candied orange peel while candies are soft. Serve candies in paper candy cups.   *Makes 24 candies*

Walnut Marzipan
Chocolates

What You'll Need

- ¾ cup (about 7½ ounces) marzipan
- ¼ cup finely ground walnuts
- 1 tablespoon dark rum
- 10 ounces milk chocolate
- About 30 walnut halves
- Colorful paper candy cups

— Variations —

For ginger filling, combine ½ cup (about 5½ ounces) marzipan, 2 tablespoons finely chopped candied ginger and 1 tablespoon dark rum; knead until smooth. Roll out as directed and cut into small squares or diamonds. Coat each piece with melted dark chocolate; top with a piece of candied ginger and let set.

For coffee filling, sift 1 teaspoon instant coffee over marzipan, then add 1 tablespoon coffee liqueur; knead until smooth. Proceed as directed, garnishing each piece with a chocolate-covered coffee bean.

1. Crumble marzipan into medium mixing bowl. Add ground walnuts and dark rum.

2. Using hands or strong fork, knead mixture until smooth and well combined.

3. Place mixture between 2 sheets of plastic wrap or waxed paper; roll out to ½-inch-thick rectangle.

4. Carefully peel off plastic wrap. With sharp knife, neatly cut candy into 1-inch squares.

5. In top of double boiler or bowl set over simmering water, melt chocolate. Dip squares in chocolate to coat.

6. Transfer candy to wire rack; top each with walnut half and let set. Place each chocolate in paper candy cup.

Makes 2½ dozen marzipan chocolates

Delicious Cherry Truffles

What You'll Need

- 8 squares (8 ounces) milk chocolate
- ½ cup heavy cream
- 4 tablespoons butter
- 3 tablespoons kirsch (cherry brandy)
- 1 tablespoon cocoa
- ½ teaspoon cinnamon

— *Quick Tips* —

For the best flavor and texture, use only fresh cream and butter. Be sure to prepare the truffle paste ahead of time, because it has to cool for at least 8 hours before it can be shaped. It is essential to shape the truffle paste quickly; otherwise, you will end up with a lot of chocolate on your hands. If you prefer, roll the truffles in grated chocolate instead of cocoa and cinnamon. Truffles taste best when they are fresh, but they can be kept in the refrigerator for about 2 weeks.

1. Coarsely chop chocolate with large, sharp knife. Avoid moisture by working on clean, dry cutting board.

2. Heat cream until hot. Remove from heat; add chocolate and butter and stir until melted and smooth.

3. Add kirsch to chocolate mixture; stir to combine. Cover and refrigerate about 8 hours or until mixture is thick enough to shape.

4. In shallow dish, mix cocoa and cinnamon. Scoop walnut-sized pieces from chocolate mixture with teaspoon.

5. With your hands, rapidly form pieces into 1- to 1½-inch balls. Work quickly to avoid melting chocolate.

6. Gently roll truffles in cocoa mixture until completely coated. Chill briefly; set aside in cool place. Serve in multicolored, pleated paper candy cups.
Makes about 2 dozen truffles

Recipe Index

METRIC CONVERSION CHART

VOLUME MEASUREMENTS (dry)

⅛ teaspoon = 0.5 mL
¼ teaspoon = 1 mL
½ teaspoon = 2 mL
¾ teaspoon = 4 mL
1 teaspoon = 5 mL
1 tablespoon = 15 mL
2 tablespoons = 30 mL
¼ cup = 60 mL
⅓ cup = 75 mL
½ cup = 125 mL
⅔ cup = 150 mL
¾ cup = 175 mL
1 cup = 250 mL
2 cups = 1 pint = 500 mL
3 cups = 750 mL
4 cups = 1 quart = 1 L

VOLUME MEASUREMENTS (fluid)

1 fluid ounce (2 tablespoons) = 30 mL
4 fluid ounces (½ cup) = 125 mL
8 fluid ounces (1 cup) = 250 mL
12 fluid ounces (1½ cups) = 375 mL
16 fluid ounces (2 cups) = 500 mL

WEIGHTS (mass)

½ ounce = 15 g
1 ounce = 30 g
3 ounces = 90 g
4 ounces = 120 g
8 ounces = 225 g
10 ounces = 285 g
12 ounces = 360 g
16 ounces = 1 pound = 450 g

DIMENSIONS

1/16 inch = 2 mm
⅛ inch = 3 mm
¼ inch = 6 mm
½ inch = 1.5 cm
¾ inch = 2 cm
1 inch = 2.5 cm

OVEN TEMPERATURES

250°F = 120°C
275°F = 140°C
300°F = 150°C
325°F = 160°C
350°F = 180°C
375°F = 190°C
400°F = 200°C
425°F = 220°C
450°F = 230°C

BAKING PAN SIZES

Utensil	Size in Inches/Quarts	Metric Volume	Size in Centimeters
Baking or Cake Pan (square or rectangular)	8×8×2	2 L	20×20×5
	9×9×2	2.5 L	23×23×5
	12×8×2	3 L	30×20×5
	13×9×2	3.5 L	33×23×5
Loaf Pan	8×4×3	1.5 L	20×10×7
	9×5×3	2 L	23×13×7
Round Layer Cake Pan	8×1½	1.2 L	20×4
	9×1½	1.5 L	23×4
Pie Plate	8×1¼	750 mL	20×3
	9×1¼	1 L	23×3
Baking Dish or Casserole	1 quart	1 L	—
	1½ quart	1.5 L	—
	2 quart	2 L	—